T5-ANA-019

CLASSIC
FILM
SCRIPTS

MOTHER

a film by V. I. Pudovkin

EARTH

a film by Alexander Dovzhenko

Lorrimer Publishing, London

All rights reserved including the right
of reproduction in whole or in part in any form
This edition copyright © 1973 by Lorrimer Publishing Limited
Published by Lorrimer Publishing Limited
47 Dean Street, London W1
First printing

SBN paper 900855 81 9
      cloth 900855 82 7

This edition is not for sale in the United States of America,
its territories, possessions, protectorates, mandated territories,
the Philippines or the Dominion of Canada

Manufactured in Great Britain by Villiers Publications Ltd,
London NW5

CONTENTS

A NOTE ON THIS EDITION

The versions of the two great Russian classics presented here are taken from the scenarios originally published in Russia and intended in each case as a literary rendering of the film. Any significant divergences between the scenario and the version of the film now available to English or American viewers are indicated by footnotes in the text.

The version of *Mother*, translated by Gillon R. Aitken, is taken from a volume published in Russia in 1935.

The version of *Earth*, translated by Diana Matias, is taken from a volume entitled *Zemlya: Knyiga-Film*, edited by Yu. Solntseva and G. Maryamov, published in Moscow in 1966.

ACKNOWLEDGMENTS

Acknowledgments and thanks are due to Contemporary Films Ltd., for providing a print of *Mother*, and to the National Film Archive for making available a print of *Earth*.

MOTHER

CREDITS:

Scenario by	Nathan Zarkhy
Based on the novel by	Maxim Gorky
Directed by	Vsevolod Pudovkin
Produced by	Mezhrabpom-Rus
Photography	Anatoli Golovnya
Art director	Sergei Kozlovsky
Assistant directors	Mikhail Doller
	V. I. Strauss
Music (added in 1935)	S. Blok
Length	1,800 metres
First shown in Russia	11th October 1926

CAST:

The mother	Vera Baranovskaya
Vlasov, her husband	A. Tchistyakov
Pavel, her son	Nikolai Batalov
Isaika Gorbov, the foreman	Alexander Savitsky
Vesovshchikov, Pavel's friend	Ivan Koval-Samborsky
Anna, a girl student	Anna Zemtsova
A police officer	Vsevolod Pudovkin
Misha	N. Vidonov

7

The basic theme of this scenario — how a 'mother' joins the revolutionary movement — is taken from M. Gorky's novel of the same name. However, the course of the story and of the characters is developed independently of the novel — from the cause of the mother's change of heart and her unintentional treachery to her death in the demonstration.

In an historical and actual sense, the scenario departs from Gorky's book inasmuch as it is based on real events taking place at Tvera during 1905-1906 — the various historical sources for which include particularly the reminiscences of Comrade Smirnov, which appeared in *Pravda* on 10th January 1926.

From such real events come the unsuccessful attempt to organise a strike (Part Two), the killing of an agitator, etc.; and, indeed, the whole story of the demonstration against the prison, culminating in its downfall.

N. Zarkhy, 1926

Mother was written some eight years ago. The progress of our art since that time has been brilliant and highly educative. It may be, therefore, that much in the scenario and its style of presentation will now seem out-of-date or naive. I have not deemed it necessary, however, to introduce changes or amendments. Let the scenario speak for itself.

N. Z., December 1934

PART ONE

The outlines of a large factory are dimly visible through a warm, winter fog. The factory chimneys loom in silhouette against the evening sky.

Evening. It is snowing. A deserted workers' street on the outskirts of a small provincial town. Two parallel rows of mean, terraced houses recede into the fog.

In the foreground — an oil street lamp, illuminating the gloomy, statuesque figure of a motionless policeman.

The door of one of the houses, the tavern, is flung open, and a couple of men, amid clouds of steam, are thrown out into the street.

Unable to support himself on his feet, one falls into a snowdrift.

The other, a huge, dark shape, stands still for a moment, then starts forward unsteadily.

... He pauses by the lamp and leans against it. He peers ahead with glazed, drunken eyes.

The face of the policeman turns in his direction.

The drunk — the locksmith Vlasov — turns round and stumbles backwards.

Waving his long arms foolishly, he staggers away and disappears in the evening fog.

AS IS OFTEN THE CASE:
THE MOTHER — DOWNTRODDEN,
THE FATHER — A DRUNK.

A room at Vlasov's.

Pashka[1] sleeps on the bed, his head buried in a pillow.

Bent over the sink in a dark corner — his mother ... (*Still*)

The door is opened noisily. On the threshold — Vlasov. He enters the room and looks round him with lack-lustre eyes.

The mother starts ... raises her eyes. She bends over her work again.

---

[1] The diminutive form of Pavel.

Pashka opens his eyes, rolls over onto the other side, falls asleep again . . .

Vlasov's vacant gaze moves from object to object.

It rests . . .

. . . on the wall clock, with its two chains and a flat iron hanging from one in place of a weight.

He goes up to the clock, removes the flat iron and puts it in a huge trouser pocket.

He hesitates for a moment, then picks up a stool, puts it against the wall and climbs up to take down the clock.

The mother, following him with her eyes, understands his intention. She jumps up, runs over to him and tries to knock him off the stool. The father kicks out at her . . . (*Still*)

The mother doesn't stop, but clutches at him . . .

Savage, Vlasov shouts at her:

' *Who's boss around here?* '

Pashka wakes, raises himself and watches . . .

. . . The mother pulls at the father . . .

Vlasov lifts his hands against her, and then, losing his balance, jumps down, taking the clock with him . . .

The clock smashes to pieces on the floor.

Both look dumbly at the clock.

Vlasov comes to his senses, hurls himself at the mother and strikes her.

The mother beats him off.

Pashka jumps up from the bed and rushes between them.

Vlasov, maddened by the unexpected interference of his son, strikes him so that . . .

. . . Pashka falls to the floor, but he quickly . . .

. . . jumps to his feet and seizes from the table . . .

. . . a hammer.

He waves the hammer at his father.

' *Don't dare strike my mother!* '

Vlasov is dumbfounded. There is such menace in Pashka's eyes that Vlasov lets go of his wife. Swearing coarsely, he goes to the door.

The mother crawls over the floor, picking up . . .

. . . springs and wheels from the broken clock.

The street. The doors of the tavern are wide, invitingly open. Every now and then people go in.

The tavern is full of people. Everywhere is drunken merriment. Accordions are being played noisily . . .

A small but hearty group are drinking together in a special room. Among them is the foreman, Isaika Gorbov, one of the leaders of the Black Hundreders[1] gathered in the room. A few mournful drunkards. Two or three workers from the factory who belong to the 'solidarity' group. They have all drunk heavily, but not so much that they cannot discuss their affairs. They listen attentively to Gorbov, each expressing his approval and agreement.

Gorbov speaks weightily, commandingly:

'*We surround . . . Stop . . . organising the strike . . . Stir up trouble . . . One, two, three . . . !*'

A shout of drunken approval.

Together the kulaks[2] strike at the air as if already beating someone up . . . A roar . . .

The public part of the tavern. Vlasov enters . . . He goes to the counter . . . He takes the iron from his pocket and silently holds it out . . .

. . . to the corpulent innkeeper, who looks at the iron and returns it to Vlasov: 'Sorry, I can't take it'.

Vlasov gives him a savage look. The innkeeper turns away.

Vlasov aimlessly turns the iron over in his hands . . . Then he crashes it down on the counter . . . so that the crockery jumps.

He shouts threateningly:

'*You won't take it?*'

Those in the special room cock an ear as they hear a row beginning. (*Still*) Isaika Gorbov opens the door and sees Vlasov. He turns back into the room and calls out:

'*Vlasov . . . Fetch him here, we want a man.*'

One of the company gets up, takes a glass of vodka with him, and goes into the public part of the tavern.

Vlasov holds the iron over the innkeeper's head.

The man approaches him and seizes his arm from behind.

Vlasov turns round in fury and yells:

---

1 Members of the Black Hundred, a virulent right-wing, anti-Jewish society.
2 Well-to-do peasants.

' Who wants to get killed, then?'

He sees the glass of vodka held out to him and lowers his uplifted hand with the iron in it. He seizes the glass and drinks thirstily.

Vlasov's face softens. He hugs the man who brought the drink — a friend.

Arm in arm, they go into the separate room.

In the separate room. The company around the table greets Vlasov. They regale him. They drink . . . and Vlasov sheds drunken tears. *(Still)*

' Friends . . . Comrades . . . Dear friends.'

The accordions play . . . All is happy in the tavern.

The street. Snow as before.

A dark figure, trying to avoid the attention of passers-by, approaches the Vlasov house. The figure taps cautiously on a little window.

It is late for the Vlasov household. The mother sleeps on the bed.

Pashka is not yet asleep. He is preparing to go to bed — undressing . . . He hears the knock.

He goes over to the window and looks out into the dark, wintry street . . .

. . . And he quickly puts on his boots and overcoat and goes out.

In the doorway of the Vlasov house stands the dark figure of a young girl — Anna. She has come to see Pashka.

Pashka goes out, greets her. He questions her anxiously.

Anna hands him a small, heavy package.

' It's not safe with us. You hide it, Pavel.'

Pavel takes the package and stows it under his coat.

' All right.'

They say good-bye. Anna walks away. Pashka goes back into the house.

Pashka enters the room. He steals across the room, trying not to make the floorboards creak. He looks down . . .

. . . at his sleeping mother. She stirs in her sleep.

Pashka freezes on the spot. He looks . . .

. . . at his sleeping mother.

He tiptoes over to the corner of the room. He kneels down on

the floor. Carefully he takes up a floorboard . . .
The mother wakes. She opens her eyes . . . and looks across . . .
(*Still*)
Out of focus — the blurred shape of Pashka putting the package under the floorboard. (*Still*)
The mother raises herself . . . She looks across the room, but after her heavy sleep she cannot see properly . . . She closes her eyes and goes back to sleep again . . .
Anna's small figure retreats across a deserted, snowy field.[1]

PART TWO

Early morning. The factory hooter sounds for work.
The factory hasn't come to life yet.
A watchman opens the heavy factory gates.
A long, protracted blast on the hooter.
The little town hasn't come to life yet.
The mother, carrying a couple of full buckets, goes out of the door.
The hooter cuts off, then sounds again.
A hand hastily nails an announcement to the factory fence. A young man starts in alarm at the din of the hooter. He looks hurriedly around him, and, without completing his task, so that the announcement flaps in the wind, he quickly strides away . . .
. . . from the street, now coming to life, and along which the first workers are heading towards the factory.
The hooter sounds.
In a dark shed, in the light of an oil lamp, a group of murky figures — yesterday's drunks, Vlasov's ' friends '. They are armed with knuckle-dusters, weighted straps and sandbags.
Vlasov's house. Vlasov, dour-faced after the previous evening's drinking, prepares to leave.
The mother comes in. She puts down the buckets. Vlasov picks up a ladle and scoops some water from one of the buckets

---

[1] The film includes at this point a scene not mentioned in the scenario, featuring Anna and Pashka. The group of revolutionary workers to which they belong meets in the countryside and there is an exchange of the revolutionary leaflets which are to be smuggled into the factory.

13

brought by the mother. He drinks avidly.

A worker of insignificant appearance, one of the Black Hundreders, knocks insistently at the window of Vlasov's house.

Vlasov hears the knock. He throws down the ladle. He goes out. Vlasov goes up to the man in the doorway.

The man asks angrily:

'*What's keeping you? It's long since time.*'

The two men walk quickly up the street.

The dark shed. Those seated inside turn at a knock at the door. Vlasov enters with his friend.

Isaika Gorbov shows Vlasov the weapons — knuckle-dusters, straps and sandbags: 'Take your pick'.

Vlasov chooses a weighted strap. He weighs it in his hand, swings it through the air and crashes it down on the table . . . He is satisfied with the result.

The hooter continues to sound.

They leave the shed in a crowd.

They walk down the street towards the factory . . . (*Still*)

The watchman at the factory gates. They go up to him.

'*Off you go, Erofeitch. The others'll take over watch from you now.*'

The old watchman protests: he cannot desert his post.

Gorbov insists. The old man is stubborn.

Gorbov looks round. He says to someone standing by:

'*Run and get Ivan Firsytch.*'

A man runs off to fetch Ivan Firsytch . . . The rest of them stay where they are.

In the yard. Ivan Firsytch is there. He is on the administrative staff of the factory.

The man sent to fetch him runs up and speaks to him . . . They walk together towards the gates.

Gorbov, pointing at the old watchman, complains to Ivan Firsytch.

Ivan Firsytch orders the watchman to go. The old man obeys unwillingly.

The old man walks away.

Gorbov puts two new guards on the gates: they are from his gang.

Gorbov and the rest walk on.

The factory yard. By the huge factory doors Gorbov gives orders to two further men chosen by him.

The two men stay in the yard by the doors. The rest go on into the factory building.

In the factory. Work has already started . . .

Hardly anyone looks up at the new arrivals, who disperse quickly to their places not far from the entrance, and set to work . . .

A small group of some fifteen workers approaches the factory gates. Among them are Pashka, Anna and the young man who nailed up the announcement.

The group passes through the gates, heading across the yard for the factory doors.

The two guards on the gates lock them.

The two other guards posted by Gorbov at the factory doors exchange glances. And when . . .

. . . the entire group has gone through the factory doors . . .

. . . they slam the heavy doors shut and lock them from the outside.

THE TRAP.

The factory. The entire group of workers is inside.

The Black Hundreders look at one another. Isaika looks to one side.

Isaika gives a sign.

The Black Hundreders leave their places and inconspicuously begin to surround those who have come in . . .

Pashka detaches himself from his group.

Vlasov's face, stunned by surprise. He had not expected to see Pashka.

' *Pashka! My son!* '

Pashka shouts:

' *Comrades! Stop work . . .* '

At this moment the Black Hundreders surround the new arrivals.

' *Stop . . . !* '

Not a movement in the factory . . .

The newcomers have been caught off guard. But Pashka comes to his senses:

'Comrades, help us . . . !' (*Still*)

There is a stir among the workers.

The Black Hundreders hurl themselves at the newcomers. A fight . . .

Vlasov rushes angrily towards Pashka.

The fight . . . Some of the workers rush up to help . . .

Noticing them, Gorbov threatens them with a revolver snatched from his pocket.

' *Get back, you devils!* '

Pashka strikes Gorbov. Gorbov groans, collapses . . .

Under pressure from the Black Hundreders, the strikers are forced towards the doors.

(*Still*)

But the doors are locked, and the efforts of the retreating men to break through them are unsuccessful.

In the struggle Anna falls. Pashka drags her to another way out on the opposite side. A number of others follow after them. One of the workers opens the doors . . . Anna, the other workers, Pashka and the lad who had nailed up the announcement rush through.

The factory yard . . . Anna, Pashka and the others burst through the doors. They run round the yard . . . towards the other gates.

Vlasov chases after them:

' *Stop, you son of a bitch!* '

The gates are locked.

Two of the workers leap over the fence. Pashka helps Anna to climb up.

Anna climbs the fence and jumps down.

Vlasov runs up to the fence.

Pashka climbs up the fence.

Vlasov, running up, seizes him by the leg.

Pashka, on top of the fence, kicks out.

Vlasov, enraged, does not let go, hitting out at his son violently.

' *So you're with them, are you?* '

Pashka manages to kick Vlasov.

Vlasov falls.

Pashka jumps off the fence and runs after the disappearing figure of Anna and the limping young man.

Shots of the struggle in the factory intersperse with shots of

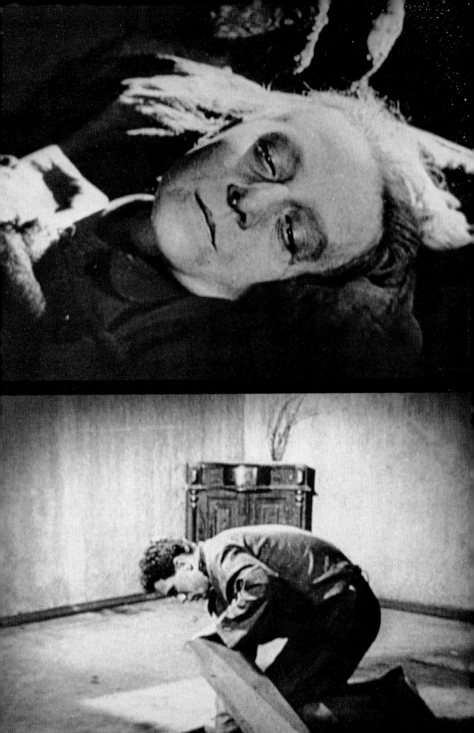

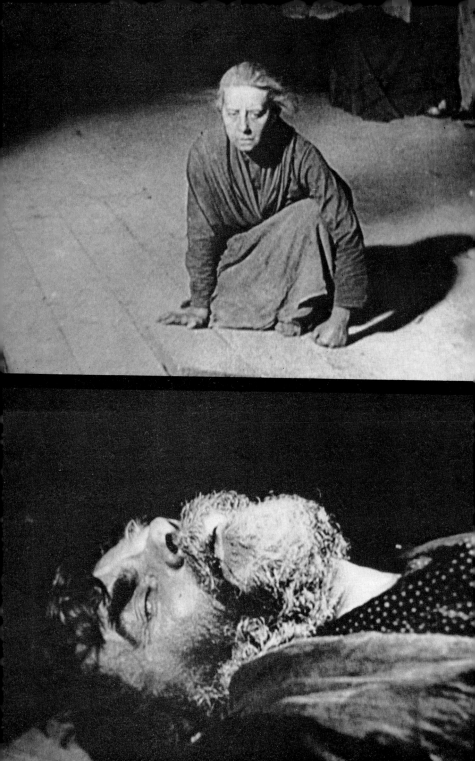

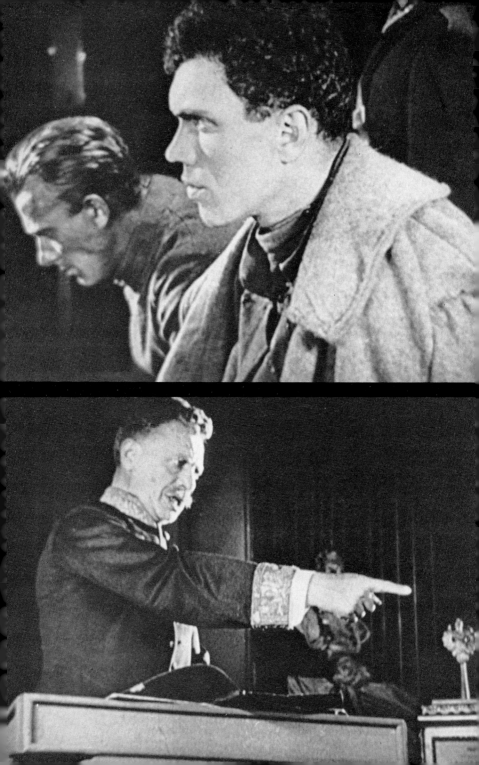

Pashka and the others.

Vlasov jumps to his feet, climbs over the fence and runs off in pursuit.

The outskirts of the town. The fleeing trio running, it seems, towards ... a policeman and a group of Black Hundreders ... They stop and begin to run back.

But from this direction, running towards them, come Vlasov and some other Black Hundreders who have joined him.

Pashka, Anna and the young man reach the door of the tavern. Their pursuers are catching up with them.

Pashka pushes open the door of the tavern. The three of them run in ...

Beating at the door. Pashka has managed to fix the hook.

The tavern is empty, the tables upended.

The frightened innkeeper runs in through an inner door behind the counter.

Vlasov and the others hammer at the door of the tavern.

The innkeeper, trying to bar his way, is sent flying by Pashka. Anna, followed by Pashka, rushes through the inner door behind the counter.

The innkeeper leaps to his feet and falls upon the young man, who has not been able to get away. They fight.

Under pressure from the hammering, the door of the tavern bursts open. A crowd of men, led by Vlasov, rushes into the tavern.

Looking round, Vlasov sees that Pashka isn't there, and yells: ' Where's Pashka?'

The innkeeper, letting go of the young man for a moment, points to the door behind the counter.

The young man, taking advantage of the moment, rushes for the door.

His way is barred

The young man jumps onto the counter. Alarm and terror show in his eyes ...

The crowd hurls itself at him.

The young man snatches a revolver from his pocket and with trembling hand points it at ... (Still)

... his attackers. The crowd recoils ...

The enraged Vlasov, his only thought to catch Pashka, is

25

further maddened by the obstacle presented by the young man, and he picks up a stool and hurls it at ...
... the young man, who manages to duck out of the way.
The stool crashes against the wall.
Bottles and various other objects are hurled at the young man. Hunched up, white-faced but not firing his revolver, the young man turns to escape the barrage.
The hand of one of the crowd seizes his leg.
The young man slips — and as he falls, the revolver accidentally goes off ...
Vlasov rocks back and falls ...
Animal-like, the crowd falls on the young man. A struggle.
Pashka and Anna run through the back yards of the town. They pause to recover their breath. Pashka remembers.
' *Where's Misha?* '
On the floor of the tavern, from behind the throng — the savaged body of the young man, and alongside ...
... the body of the father.
Pashka and Anna run on through the back yards of the town.

PART THREE

Vlasov's house. In the corner, before an icon, the mother prays. She prays ardently, making genuflections ...
During one of these, when the mother has bowed almost to the ground, her eyes fall ... (*Still*)
... on a floorboard raised slightly above the level of the others ...
Flashback — the scene of the previous evening, observed through her sleep: Pashka is hiding a package ...
She forgets her prayers ... and goes down on her knees. She feels for the floorboard ... and raises it. Beneath is ...
... a package.
The perplexed, frightened face of the mother ... She lifts out the package and undoes it ...
In the package are arms: two or three revolvers, ammunition ...
The mother looks frightened to death ...

In terror, not daring to touch the arms, she looks at them.
Then she turns. She is confused. She does not know what to do
— whether to throw them away, carry them out of the house or
put them back . . . Suddenly she hears a noise . . . The proces-
sion bearing the body of the father is approaching the house . . .
She turns quickly and returns the package to its hiding-place.
She fits the floorboard back . . .
She gets up and looks at the door . . .
Vlasov's body is carried into the room. A crowd follows, among
it a number of women looking on with curiosity . . .
Dully, horrified, the mother looks at the procession, not moving
from her position. As if frozen, she observes the activities of
the people . . .
They lay Vlasov's body on the bed . . . The mother moves from
her position, goes over to the body.
At once, as if obeying an order, the women begin to moan.
The mother approaches the bed . . . With unseeing, dry eyes,
she looks at . . .
. . . the dead face of Vlasov. (*Still*)
And even more loudly and with even more passion, the official
mourners — old village women — weep and wail . . .

A company of dragoons enters the town.
Along the street the grey ranks of soldiers, with measured step,
in time with . . .
. . . the drummer . . .
. . . march towards the factory.
The company goes in through the factory gates.
The gloomy faces of the workers.
The officer gives an order:
' *Dismiss!* '
In the factory building, the workers setting about their work
are silent.
Ivan Firsytch, on the administrative staff of the factory, hurries
up to the officer.
A conversation. An exchange of compliments. The officer gives
his orders. Soldiers move off to various parts of the building.
A group of soldiers remains in the yard.

IN SHIPKA ALL IS PEACEFUL.

In the factory, work goes on under the watch of the military.

Vlasov's house. Late evening. The room is lit by an icon-lamp and a candle ...
... at the head of the corpse, prepared and laid out on a table moved into the corner under the icon.
Seated by the head of the corpse, at the side of the table — the unmoving, lifeless figure of the mother.
The flickering candle projects onto the walls the shadow of ...
... a number of women approaching to pay their last respects to the dead man ...
The women begin to leave.
One of them goes up to the mother and whispers:
' Keep Pashka under control. It was all his fault. He'll be the cause of his own and other people's death.' (Still)
The mother hears her in silence. And before her eyes, which wander towards the floorboard ...
... appears the package with the arms ... A heavy sigh, and the head of the mother sinks yet lower under the burden of her grievous thoughts.

The town ... A group of soldiers with an officer at its head emerges from one of the houses ... escorting a worker who has just been arrested.

Vlasov's house. Pashka comes in through the door.
He pauses on the threshold and takes in the room with his eyes.
Above the sharp profile of the dead man — the face of the mother ...
... her eyes raised towards her son ...
A heavy, oppressive, almost tangible silence in the room.
Water dripping into the hand-basin.
Pashka stands there, performs unnecessary movements ... He takes off his cap, screws it up in his hands ... He unbuttons his coat. He advances noisily into the room. He looks at his father's lifeless face ... He moves away and sits down to one side ...
Without looking at his mother, separated from him by the

28

table bearing the dead man, he asks:

' *Who killed him?* '

His mother raises her eyes. With difficulty, opening her parched lips, through which no word has passed all day, she answers:

' *Your lot . . . your lot killed him.* '

And from her eyes, the first, sparse tears.

Pashka's face darkens . . . His eyes carry to the floorboard alongside the table on which the dead man lies . . . He moves towards the floorboard.

The mother intercepts Pashka's glance. Her face clouds over, not with reproach, but with despair, the despair of a mother in fear of losing her son.

' *Why did you get involved with them, my little Pashka?* '

Pashka doesn't speak. He sniffs noisily . . . His face becomes yet more grim.

His mother heaves with silent sobs . . .

Pashka gazes unwaveringly at the floorboard . . . A moment of hesitation. Then he decides . . . He must get the package. He bends down.

His mother observes his movement . . . She gets up from her place and moves round the table . . . She grasps Pashka.

In her eyes — fear, despair and terror.

' *No, no . . . Pashka, throw them away!* '

Pashka looks darkly at her. He understands: he knows his mother.

Decisively, he pushes her aside . . .

But the mother clings all the harder to him . . . She clasps him to her convulsively.

' *Throw them away, Pashka, throw them away!* '

And the suppressed, persistent thought is torn from her — in a voice full of reproach and fear:

' *They'll kill you, they'll kill you, too, Pashka!* '

Pashka tries to free himself from his mother's restraining grasp . . .

. . . But the mother clings to him even more tightly . . . and struggles with him. She clutches his knees. She begs him, choking through her tears . . .

Pashka's face is distorted with pain . . . But he remains determined to oppose his mother . . . and she, with an unnatural strength, clings even harder.

The entrance to the house. Vesovshchikov, a young worker, one of those who had helped Pashka to organise the strike that morning, knocks insistently at the door.

In the room, they listen . . . and turn . . . Pashka frees himself and opens the door.

Vesovshchikov enters, agitated and out of breath. He sees Pashka and cries out:

' *The soldiers . . . they're on their way!* '

Pashka starts.

The mother is panic-stricken. Her fears are being realised.

Pashka hastily questions Vesovshchikov.

A detachment of soldiers, an officer at their head, approaches Vlasov's house.

They pass through the gate . . . and walk up to the entrance. In the room they hear the noise and stand as if frozen.

Through the door comes the detachment:

an officer — small, supercilious, sharp-faced . . .

. . . a number of soldiers, the policeman . . .

. . . and two witnesses from the town.

PART FOUR

The detachment comes to a halt in the doorway.

The officer takes off his cap . . . The others follow suit . . . One of the soldiers crosses himself . . .

The soldiers are disconcerted by the unusual circumstances of the search and shift soundlessly from one foot to another. There is a heavy silence . . .

. . . broken by a deep sigh from the huge, fat, clumsy policeman. This sigh seems to allow the others to relax . . .

The officer moves to the middle of the room and sits down on a stool.

He takes a piece of paper from his pocket and inspects it. (*Still*) His eyes light on Vesovshchikov, who has been following his movements with a sardonic expression.

' *Vlasov, Pavel . . .* '

The drawn face of the mother . . . holding her breath.

Vesovshchikov answers quickly, stepping forward:
' *Here!* '
Pashka pushes Vesovshchikov aside.
' *He's deceiving you. I'm Vlasov.* '
The officer frowns threateningly . . .
The face of Vesovshchikov with its sardonic expression.
The face of the mother.
The officer begins his interrogation:
' *Confess everything . . . Who led the strike . . . ? Where did you
get the arms . . . ? If you confess, nothing will happen to you . . .* '
A deathly hush. The tense faces of the people in the room.
The officer speaks again:
' *If you conceal anything, it'll be the worse for you.* '
Pashka answers in a firm voice:
' *We know nothing, we don't have any arms . . .* '
The officer looks searchingly into the face of . . .
. . . Vesovshchikov . . .
. . . and the mother.
The officer makes a sign.
The soldiers start searching.

In one of the rooms in the factory. A kind of headquarters.
Officers, soldiers . . . someone from the administrative staff . . .
Isaika Gorbov . . .
One of the Black Hundreders comes in at the door . . . He calls
Gorbov over and whispers:
' *They've caught Pashka at Vlasov's.* '
Gorbov's face lights up . . . He approaches the colonel in charge
of the search for arms . . . He reports to him, respectfully urges
him in some matter. The colonel listens attentively.
The colonel gets up and goes over to the door. Gorbov minces
after him.

At Vlasov's. The search is over. Nothing has been found. The
disappointed, tired face of the officer. He gets up from his seat.
He looks around at everybody once more.
' *You've got away lightly this time!* '
He goes over to the door, followed by the others.
Light-headed with happiness, the mother, bowing low, sees the

31

officer out.

The soldiers go out of the gate.

There they are met — by the colonel, Garbov mincing behind him.

The colonel goes up to the officer, who salutes and gives his report:

'We didn't find a thing, colonel.'

Isaika's ugly face twisted with disappointment.

The colonel looks at him.

He turns back to the officer.

'Arrest Vlasov.'

The colonel himself goes into the house, followed by the rest of them.

In the room ... Pashka and Vesovshchikov quietly exchange looks. From time to time, the mother, from her old position at the head of the corpse, looks at them.

They hear a noise and turn towards the door ...

In the doorway — the colonel, the officer and the others.

The officer points at Pashka.

'Arrest him!'

The soldiers go up to Pashka.

The mother rushes over to Pashka and attaches herself to him:

'What for, sir, what for?'

The colonel answers:

'Because he won't confess. Now it'll be much worse for him.'

The soldiers try to push the mother away from Pashka.

The mother will not go.

One of the soldiers brandishes his scabbard at her.

Pashka seizes his arm.

'Don't dare do that!'

He pushes the soldier, causing him to stagger.

The colonel screams:

'Tie the villain up!'

They seize Pashka's arms and pinion them behind his back.

In total terror, the mother ...

'Sir, sir ...!'

The colonel looks the mother full in the face — weightily, significantly.

'If he tells us who the instigators are ... where they got the

arms . . . then all will be forgiven.'
In her fear, not realising what she is doing the mother cries out:
' He'll confess everything, sir — everything.'
She turns to Pashka.
' Tell them, Pashka.'
A deathly hush.
Faces staring tensely at Pashka . . .
Pashka's drained face, his lips trembling . . .
He hasn't the strength to utter a word.
The angry face of Vesovshchikov, ready to strike the mother.
The face of the dead man.
The mother no longer knows what she is doing. With feverish movements she bends towards the floor.
She holds everyone's gaze.
Pashka tries to rush over to her, but he is forcibly held back.
The mother raises the floorboard and takes out the package.
Smiling pitifully through her tears, she hands it to the colonel.
' Take it, sir.'
The colonel almost grabs the package from her hands. He opens it and sees . . .
. . . the revolver, the ammunition. He looks up . . .
. . . at Pashka, who looks back with unseeing eyes,
. . . at Vesovshchikov, his eyes downcast,
. . . at the mother, pitiful and distraught.
The colonel makes a sign with his eyes.
The soldiers bind Vesovshchikov's hands.
The colonel goes over to Pashka and strikes him in the face with the back of his hand.
Pashka rocks back.
The face of the mother . . . Her trembling lips whisper, as if in a dream.
' Sir . . . sir . . . '
The soldiers surround Pashka and Vesovshchikov and lead them away.
The mother rushes after them.
One of the soldiers pushes her back roughly.
' Get back! '
Her hand outstretched, in utter despair, the mother gazes at the departing figures.

' Sir ... sir ...'

The room empties.

In utter despair, her hand outstretched, an unfinished sentence on her lips, the mother stands as if frozen.

A shot of — snowflakes falling in a gentle flurry onto her outstretched hands ...

A shot of — great, swirling snowflakes — giving way to — a desolate, snowbound, winter landscape.

PART FIVE

Early morning. A series of shots of — the dawn.

On the edge of the town, high above a steep-banked river, a dark prison building.

Under the walls of the prison, trying not to be seen by the sentries who parade the walls at a slow, regular pace, stands the mother.

A sentry draws near to her from round a corner.

The mother runs down to the river bank and hides behind a stunted shrub, waiting for the sentry to pass.

The sentry passes by.

The mother comes out from behind the shrub.

She looks up intently at ...

... a barred window on the third floor of the prison ...

In a cell for one person — Pashka ... He goes over to the window ... He looks out ...

The mother sees Pashka at the window. She begins to feel agitated. She is afraid that Pashka will not see her. She tries to attract his attention ...

In the cell, Pashka sees the mother ... He smiles ... He opens the tiny window and sticks his hand through.

The mother is overjoyed ... Forgetting her caution, she steps forward, closer to the wall, in order to be able to talk to Pashka.

The approaching sentry notices her ... He shouts to the mother, bringing up his rifle.

The mother hears the shout of the sentry ... She waves to Pashka.

The sentry moves towards her, chases her away ...

The sentry pushing her, the mother slowly walks away, every moment looking back over her shoulder . . .
Pashka shouts something out of the window.
Hearing the shout, the sentry turns towards him . . . He raises his rifle.
' Get back! '
Pashka moves away from the window.
Weeping, the mother walks away.

The same morning. The factory gates. Workers pass through the gates on their way to work.
Three men stand just inside the gates: Isaika on one side, two of his henchmen on the other.
A number of workers pass unobstructed through the gates.
Isaika exchanges winks with . . .
. . . his henchmen. All three wait attentively. Their eyes are skinned for . . .
. . . one worker.
A worker comes up to the gates and draws level with Isaika.
Isaika nods his head in answer to the enquiring look of one of the henchmen.
The henchman stops the worker. He takes him, resisting, aside. With the aid of the second henchman, he searches the worker. In spite of the worker's protests, they frisk him all over, feel in his pocket and under his shirt.
The incident is watched with curiosity by a long queue of tradeswomen, buckets and baskets in their hands, standing inside the factory yard by the fence.
The gloomy faces of the passing workers. The angry, frustrated looks of the volunteer searchers in the direction of the workers. They find nothing on the worker . . . They let him go.
Swearing and buttoning up his things as he goes, the man passes on.
The three return to their posts, watching the workers sharply as they enter.

Anna's room. A typical student's room . . . The backs of two heads bent over a newspaper: those of Anna and one of her friends.

The newspaper. The text. A finger underlining a line of the text with its nail . . .

CONSPIRACY UNCOVERED. ARMS FOUND WITH ONE OF THE CONSPIRATORS . . . CHARGED ACCORDING TO CLAUSE* WITH THREATENING . . .

They turn towards . . .
. . . the mother, who enters the room.
The mother greets them. Tired, she sits down on a chair in the corner of the room . . .

At the factory gates . . . Two workers pass through the gates . . .
Isaika makes a sign in the direction of one of them.
The worker is surrounded . . .
The confused face of the worker, whom they take to one side.
They begin to search him.
The second worker, seeing that the first has been seized, suddenly begins to increase his pace, obviously hoping that he will catch Isaika's attention.
Indeed, Isaika notices the suspicious behaviour of the worker and runs after him.
' *Stop!* '
Isaika races off in pursuit of the man.
One of his henchmen, abandoning the worker being searched, runs after them.
They both run after the second worker, who takes to his heels. Across the courtyard, past the factory building, around the factory yard . . .
The other searcher finds some sort of package under the shirt of the first worker. He lays hold of him and tries to pull out the package.
The first worker breaks away from the searcher. The searcher grabs him. A short struggle. The searcher lands a heavy blow. His forehead cut, the worker still manages to stay on his feet, and he pushes the searcher to the ground. He runs off . . .
He runs out of the gates . . .
The searcher jumps up . . .
' *Stop him!* '
He sets off in pursuit . . .

36

As if by accident, the workers at the gates obstruct his way . . .
Swearing, the searcher tries to elbow his way through.
One of the workers, unnoticed, trips him up.
The searcher falls down. He swears, tries to get up, falls down again.
Suppressed laughter . . .
The first worker is already a long way off.
Isaika and the other searcher overtake the second worker. They seize him.
' *Stop!* '
The second worker resists. He tries to get away, but they hold him back. Triumphant, they search him with great care.
But their expressions of malevolent triumph gradually evaporate. They find nothing of suspicion on their ' suspicious ' worker.
Isaika asks angrily:
' *What were you running for, you swine?* '
The worker grins maliciously.
' *Aren't we allowed to run, then?* '
Furious, Isaika shakes his fist at him.

Anna's room. The mother is alone in the room . . . As before, she sits on the chair, sunk deep in her unhappy thoughts.
The first worker knocks at Anna's door.
The mother opens the door.
The first worker comes in, out of breath, half-dead from his wound.
The mother looks at him in alarm . . .
He passes into the room, slumps heavily into a chair.
The mother notices a trickle of blood coming from below the cap pulled down over his eyes . . . She is greatly agitated.
She takes off his cap. She runs from the room, returning with a towel and a bowl of water.
With all the gentleness she is capable of, she washes the wound and binds his head.
She leads him over to a small leather couch and lays him down.
The worker smiles gratefully at the mother . . .
' *Thank you, Nilovna . . .* '
The sharp face of the mother.
' *You lie there, young man.* '

Quietly she murmurs:
'I have a son ... like you ...'
A package falls out from under the worker's shirt, unbuttoned over his chest ... The mother picks up the leaflets which have scattered everywhere.
The worker sees what has happened ... Guiltily, he points at the leaflets.
'Don't take them. They're looking for them.'
The mother looks at him. Then, moved by some impulse, she begins to thrust the leaflets into her bosom.
The worker watches her, astonished.
Anna appears at the door. She stops, and she too looks at the mother in amazement.
Confused by their looks, excusing herself clumsily, the mother says:
'I ... I'll take them ...'

A few days later.
Early morning again at the factory gates ... Workers walk through the gates ...
They are all, without exception, being thoroughly searched.
A covered bucket in one hand, a basket in the other, the mother walks up to the gates.
Isaika stops her.
'Where are you going?'
The mother points at her basket and answers harshly:
'I've got to live on something, Isai Glebitch ... There's no-one to feed me now.'
Isaika regards her suspiciously. He uncovers the bucket.
The smell of hot food — liver, sausages — reaches his nose
'Pass.'
The mother goes through ... She breathes more easily now, even smiles.
The mother takes her place among the other tradeswomen.
There is a lively trade for her goods. The workers buy from her, and joke sympathetically ...
One worker approaches her. He looks at the mother questioningly.
The mother answers him with her eyes ... The worker leans

down towards the bucket, chooses some liver.
And into his pocket, unnoticed, he thrusts the handful of leaflets
surreptitiously passed to him by the mother . . .
He stands up, smiles, eats . . .
' *Beautifully cooked, Nilovna* . . . '
A happy, fulfilled smile on the excited face of the mother, who
continues cheerfully to sell her goods . . .

THE DAY OF THE TRIAL.

The two-headed eagle on the pediment of the court-house . . .
. . . The mirror of justice.
The inscription:

A FAIR, SWIFT AND MERCIFUL TRIAL.

In the court-room.
On the public benches — the mother, her neck stretched
forward, her eyes hungrily seeking her son.
A portrait of the Tsar with sceptre and orb.
The judges' table unoccupied.
A police-officer at the door.
Two soldiers, with bayonets fixed, by the empty dock.

THE JUDGES.

The judges enter. Brilliantly uniformed with high collars
propping up their heads. Majestic representatives of the state
judiciary.

THE PROSECUTION.

The public prosecutor . . . Majestic representative of the state
prosecutor.

THE WITNESSES FOR THE PROSECUTION.

A gallery filled with Black Hundreders.
The face of the judge. He speaks.

THE DEFENCE.

A sad, insignificant, submissive figure . . . representative of the
state defender. He jumps to his feet . . .

A reverential bow towards the judges.

THE WITNESSES FOR THE DEFENCE.

An empty bench.

THE DEFENDANTS.

A bayonet, a soldier, a bayonet, a soldier.
Pashka, Vesovshchikov. (*Still*)
The mother . . .
The court stands.
' *By order of His Imperial Majesty . . .* '
The court stands.
The state defender jumps to his feet.
The public stands.
Frightened, the mother continues to sit.
The portrait of the Tsar with sceptre and orb . . .
In the square outside the court-house. Mounted policemen
disperse the crowd . . .

THE COURT PROCEEDINGS.

The public prosecutor speaks. (*Still*)

THIS EVIDENCE.

Guarded by a soldier — the revolvers, the ammunition . . .
Attending pathetically to the words of the public prosecutor,
the mother shifts her gaze in confusion from the public
prosecutor to . . .
. . . the witnesses, and to . . .
. . . the sullen face of Pashka.
The judge speaks.
' *The defence . . .* '
The state defender jumps up nervously.
' *I have nothing to . . .* '
He sits down, bites his moustache.
Pashka looks at him.
In the square outside . . . The police stand motionless. Here
and there, in corners of the square, groups of curious people . . .

THE SENTENCE.

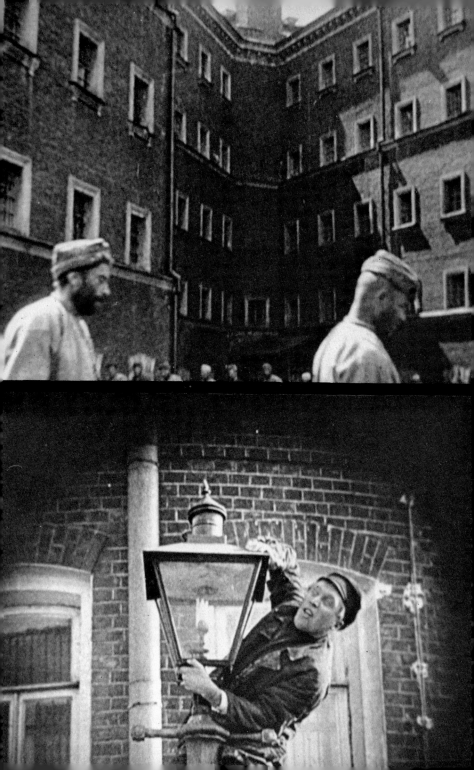

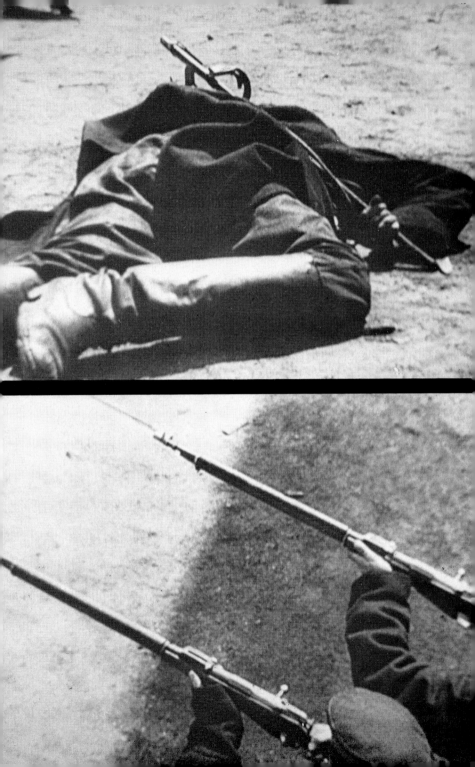

The president and the court stand.
The public and the others stand.
' In the name of His Imperial Majesty . . . '
The portrait of the Tsar.
' . . . unlimited hard labour . . . '
The mother . . .
Vesovshchikov . . .
Pashka . . .
The mother cries out:
' Where is justice? '
A police-officer and a number of soldiers force their way
through the public towards the mother . . .
The mother cries out.
In the square outside the court-house . . . A police-officer comes
out through the doors of the court-house. He calls out.
A prison carriage with escort drives up.
From behind a corner — the mother.
Pashka in the middle of the escort.
The mother rushes forward towards him.
The soldiers are disconcerted.
The mother clutches at Pashka.
' Forgive me, Pashka! '
Pashka reaches out to his mother.
A soldier drags him away.
Another soldier, in confusion, raises his rifle butt against the
mother.
Restrained in this way, not knowing what to do, she looks
round helplessly.
Members of the escort run up and drag the mother away . . .
They lead Pashka to the carriage . . . make him sit down . . .
The carriage drives off.

PART SIX

Spring has entered its full season. The snow yields to the rays
of the sun and forms into rushing streams.
The pressure of water seeking escape has broken up the icy
crust of the river, which threatens at every moment to burst its

banks — a sequence of shots.

In the factory yard, filled with striking workers — a meeting . . .
None of the administrative staff, no soldiers . . .

An earlier strike attempt has failed. Now, the attempt succeeds . . .

Hiding in one of the offices on the top floor of the factory building — Isaika and a companion.

Taking care to avoid the attention of the workers in the yard below, they watch through a narrow window.

THE MEETING.

One of the men, late to join the workers below, runs along the corridor past Isaika's hiding-place.

Isaika and his companion hear his footsteps . . . Terrified, holding their breath, they hide themselves . . .

The worker passes by.

They breathe again in relief and creep back to the window . . .
The meeting . . . A speaker . . . He calls out:

' *The first thing to do is to go to the prison and demand the release of our wrongly sentenced comrades.*'

Loud expressions of support from the workers.

The sullen faces of Isaika and his companion . . .

Bitter to them is the knowledge of their powerlessness in the face of the vast and solid strength of the workers . . .

The meeting goes on . . .

In the prison.

The mother is on a visit to Pashka. A heavy iron grille separates the mother from Pashka.

They stand in silence, looking at each other. They exchange a few words.

The prison guard, foolish-looking and sleepy.

Seizing an opportunity, the mother cautiously gropes for Pashka's hand. A note passes from her fingers to his.

The guard yawns enormously.

Pashka feels the note in his hand. A faint smile on the mother's face.

The guard turns towards them.

' *Visit's over.*'

The mother starts at the words. She looks troubled. She says good-bye.
The guard goes up to Pashka. He touches him on the shoulder.
(*Still*) Pashka gives a last glance at his mother. He smiles.
' *Thank you, mother.*'
Pashka goes out with the guard.
They walk along the prison corridor, disappear from sight.
The mother walks across the prison yard.
The heavy prison gates swing to behind her . . .
The face of a guard looking through the peephole of a prison cell.
Pashka alone in the cell. He looks unconcerned.
The guard moves away.
Pashka opens his hand and unfolds the carefully folded note.
His back to the door, he reads:

THE DEMONSTRATION WILL MOVE TOWARDS THE PRISON AT ELEVEN O'CLOCK, ROUND ABOUT YOUR EXERCISE TIME. TAKE ADVANTAGE OF THE DIS-TURBANCE . . . BY THE WALL ON THE RIGHT IS THE LAMPLIGHTER'S LADDER. ROUND THE COR-NER A SLEDGE . . .

Pashka reads through to the end. His whole being trembles with hope. He cannot contain his emotion . . .
He makes a few happy movements.
Suddenly he starts to sing — loudly, excitedly, joyfully . . .
All anxiety forgotten in his emotion, Pashka sings.
In the corridor a guard hears the singing. He listens, then goes up to Pashka's cell.
The guard at the peephole. He sees Pashka singing. He yells:
' *Stop that racket!* '
Pashka starts, is silent.
The guard shouts at him:
' *For that you get no exercise today.*'
Pashka is stunned . . . When the guard moves away from the peephole, he bursts into tears like a child.

Spring in the air.
Ice floating down the river.

The demonstration moves through the open factory gates into the street.

At the other end of the street, an old acquaintaince — the policeman on duty — watches the demonstration as it moves through the gates . . .

He experiences a brief struggle between duty and fear for his own skin — and his majestic tread gradually changes to a jog trot, then to a run, at full speed, all his old fat policeman's dignity lost.

People pour out into the street from houses on every side. Some join the demonstration. Some, the timid, stay close to their doors . . .

. . . and look on in alarm.

Getting ever larger and larger, the demonstration moves on.

A council of war in ' His Excellency's ' office.

One of the senior members of the administrative staff of the factory reports on the events . . .

' His Excellency ', decisive and cold-blooded, orders:

' *Don't spare the bullets!* '

The faces of the depressed officials brighten at the decisive words of ' His Excellency '.

The dashing colonel of dragoons bows respectfully. He leaves the council to carry out his battle orders.

New columns of workers from other factories join the marching demonstration . . .

In the yard of the barracks of the dragoons.

A trumpeter sounds the muster . . . (*Still*)

The yard fills with soldiers running from the barracks . . .

Horses are led from the stables . . .

On every side preparations for the forthcoming military action go on . . .

The prison yard. The prisoners are exercising . . . They whisper among themselves . . . They disperse quickly at the sight of . . .

. . . an approaching guard . . .

One of the prisoners, looking round to see whether a guard is watching . . .

48

... pulls a cobblestone from the ground from which the snow has melted, and puts it into the trouser pocket of his prison uniform.

In a far corner two others tear bricks from a small gap in the prison wall.

Another picks up a horseshoe lying on the ground.

When the guards approach, the prisoners continue to walk round as if nothing unusual had occurred ... (*Still*)

IT HAS NOT BEEN EASY TO REACH THE PRISON.

In the way of the demonstraton, drawing near to the prison ...
... a chain of mounted policemen, blocking the way to one of the side streets down which the demonstration must go.

The worried faces of the workers at the head of the demonstration ...

The face of the mother, concerned that the demonstration has come to a halt ...

The workers evaluate their strength ... and decide to avoid a head-on collision ...

IN RETREAT.

The demonstration begins to turn back ...

The river is impassable. Ice-floe upon ice-floe ...

The mother is anxious, dejected ... She would go on alone ... But she is carried along by the tide of the people ...

The ice-floes move apart and are carried away by the current.

The prison yard. It is almost the end of the exercise period, and there is no sign of the awaited demonstration. The gloomy faces of the prisoners ...

To one side, the lamplighter trims the wick of the lamp beside the prison wall ... (*Still*)

Standing on the ladder leaning against the lamp-post, he looks over to where ...

... the demonstration is in retreat.

The perplexed face of the lamplighter.

The prisoners in the yard notice the lamplighter by the wall. The prisoners happily exchange glances, although their hopes are vanishing.

In his cell, clinging to the window, Pashka also sees the lamplighter. He paces his cell in despair . . .

In the yard the guard gives the order for the end of the exercise period:

' *Back to your cells.*'

The disappointed faces of the prisoners. They look around at each other. They move slowly towards the doors.

PART SEVEN

The demonstration retreats.

Pashka, in despair, beats his fists against the door of his cell.

The guard hears the noise and moves towards the door.

In the narrow doorway leading from the yard into the prison building, the prisoners slowly advancing towards the stairway hesitate . . .

The guard in front shouts at them.

Suddenly, the guard falls — hit by a brick thrown at his head. Dazed, he falls . . . (*Still*)

. . . and another . . .

The prisoners dash towards the exit . . .

The guards in the yard notice . . . and rush towards the prisoners.

They are met by a hail of stones . . . A struggle.

In the corridor, by Pashka's cell, the guard is maddened by the continued frenzied hammering.

' *Stop that hammering!* '

Pashka goes on hammering without a break.

The infuriated guard opens the door of the cell, with the clear intention of beating this violent prisoner to a pulp.

Tumult in the prison . . . Alarm bells . . . Frightened guards, running around aimlessly . . .

The guard who opened the door of Pashka's cell turns round, hearing the alarm.

Not losing a moment, Pashka seizes him from behind. A fight. An atmosphere of mass rebellion pervades every corner of the prison.

The prisoners break down the door of the communal cell.

They rush out along the corridor. Among them is Vesovsh-chikov.

In the yard, the prisoners begin to climb up the wall, using the ladder left by the lamplighter.

A detachment of guards runs into the yard. They open fire at the fleeing prisoners. (*Still*) A shot hits a prisoner standing on the ladder . . .

He reels . . . and falls, dragging the ladder down with him. Other prisoners, shot by the guards, lie around . . .

Vesovshchikov rushes towards Pashka's cell.

Pashka is fighting with the guard.

Vesovshchikov runs up to the guard from behind . . . and hits him on the head.

The guard falls. Pashka and Vesovshchikov flee.

They run into the corridor, along which other prisoners are running, and along which the guards advance, shooting indiscriminately.

Pashka and Vesovshchikov run along the corridor leading to the stairs to the floor below.

Guards are running up the stairs.

Pashka and Vesovshchikov run back down the corridors of the prison.

The stairway to the attic. Pashka and Vesovshchikov run up the stairway.

The guards run along the corridor, driving the fleeing prisoners back into their cells and slamming the doors behind them.

Pashka and Vesovshchikov make their way to the attic.

The guards have restored order in the corridor. Two of them run down the corridor. They reach the stairway leading to the attic. They climb up the stairway.

Pashka and Vesovshchikov hear the noise of steps. They hide under one of the beams in the dark attic.

The guards begin to search the attic.

They draw level with the beam under which Pashka hides. Pashka stops breathing.

The guards move on and go back down the stairway.

The guards have gone.

Pashka and Vesovshchikov both listen . . . They come out from under the beam. They go over to the dormer window.

Throughout the prison, the rebellion has been quelled.

Pashka crawls through the window and jumps down on to the prison wall.

Below, beneath the wall — a sentry . . .

Not noticing the sentry, whose back is towards him, Pashka clings to the wall . . .

Pashka jumps down from the wall.

The sentry sees him.

Above, Vesovshchikov, beginning to clamber through the window, sees the sentry's drawn revolver.

He shouts out.

Pashka falls to the ground.

The sentry's shot goes wide . . . He blows his whistle . . .

Having injured his foot in the jump, Pashka cannot stand up. The sentry leaps on him. A struggle . . .

Vesovshchikov comes to Pashka's help. He hurls himself at the sentry from behind.

The sentry lets go of Pashka and begins to fight with Vesovshchikov. They struggle together on the edge of the river bank, and begin to roll down it.

Guards come running through the prison gates . . .

Vesovshchikov overcomes the sentry. He gets up, looks around and sees . . .

. . . Pashka, on his feet, hobbling after him.

Vesovshchikov waves to Pashka, signalling him to follow him to the place where . . .

. . . round a corner, at the edge of a field, a wooden cart is waiting.

Anna, dressed as a peasant girl, is in the cart.

Vesovshchikov sees the guards running . . .

He races towards the cart . . .

Anna, in the cart, sees Vesovshchikov running towards her. She is all ready to drive the horse forward.

Vesovshchikov running . . . He looks back . . .

No sign of Pashka, but in full pursuit, firing as they run, guards . . .

Vesovshchikov jumps onto the cart.

' Let's go! '

Anna looks back, her eyes searching tormentedly for Pashka . . .

She sees . . .

. . . far away, by the river bank, the figure of Pashka.

The guards are racing towards the cart.

Anna urges the horse forward.

The guards, having failed to catch them, fall behind.

Anna drives the horse at a gallop across the field.

Pashka by the river . . . He stops and sees . . .

. . . the ice in the process of breaking up. He turns.

Behind — the guards in pursuit.

A moment of thought — there's no other way: Pashka jumps on to the ice . . .

The guards open fire . . .

Pashka is hit by a bullet . . .

He crawls over the ice, one hand pressed to his wounded side.

The ice bears him downstream . . .

The demonstration approaches the square, not far from the bridge.

From the other side of the bridge, towards the demonstration, but not yet visible to it, gallop the dragoons . . .

On the opposite side of the river, overcoming the pain of his wound, Pashka clutches at the back . . . and with difficulty drags himself towards the top. At the very top, he sees . . .

. . . the demonstration drawing near.

Mustering his last strength, he runs towards it.

Overhead shot — the square into which the demonstration moves, and on the other side of the bridge, the galloping dragoons.

Pashka, pouring blood, totally exhausted, runs towards the front ranks of the demonstration.

To meet him — his excited comrades . . . and first among them, his mother.

She rushes towards him . . .

. . . and into her arms she takes the dying Pashka, drained of all strength.

She bends over him . . .

The workers break ranks and surround them on every side.

The mother looks down at the lifeless face of Pashka.

She understands . . .

Almost on top of the demonstration, the dragoons appear . . .

The dragoons gallop across the bridge.

The demonstration sees the dragoons ... Consternation ... The ranks falter ...

The dragoons gallop on. At the gallop, they lift their rifles to the shoulder. They fire.

The demonstration falls back in disorder. The standard-bearer, in the front ranks of the demonstration, beside the mother, falls ... (*Still*)

The mother raises her eyes. She looks at ...

... the officer galloping at the head of his soldiers.

Her trembling hands leave the dead body of her son.

In a sudden passion, the mother seizes the fallen standard, and not knowing what she does, marches forward with it into ...

... the advancing avalanche of the dragoons.

The dragoons fall upon her. Nothing visible but the sweating flanks of the horses. It is as if the mother has been washed away in a whirlpool.

And when the oppressed, crushed demonstrators have been scattered by the dragoons, there remains ...

... in the square now empty of people ...

... under the torn standard the mother had held in her hands ...

... the two bodies of ...

... Pashka and the mother. (*Still*)

Once more — the relentless movement of ice-floes breaking up on the wide expanse of the river.

Rushing streams flow into the river. The river on the point of overflowing ...

The sun high above the square.

The tempestuous Russian spring.

EARTH

CREDITS:

Scenario by	Alexander Dovzhenko
Directed by	Alexander Dovzhenko
Produced by	Ukrainfilm, Kiev
Photography	Danylo Demutsky
Art director	Vasily Krichevsky
Assistants	Yu. Solntseva
	L. Bodik
Length	1704 metres
First shown in Russia	8th April 1930

CAST:

Opanas Trubenko	S. Shkurat
Vasil, his son	S. Svashenko
Grandfather Semyon	N. Nademsky
Natalka, Vasil's fiancée	E. Maksimova
Arkhip Belokon, a kulak	I. Franko
Khoma, his son	P. Masokha
Father Gerasim, the priest	V. Mikhailov
Kravchina-Chuprina, the Komsomol secretary	P. Petrik

Dovzhenko originally wrote the script of *Earth* in 1929 when the impact of collectivisation on the Ukrainian village was a moment of its recent history — 'a period not only of economic transformation but also of mental transformation of the whole people'. The film itself was completed the following year.

Of this first shooting script only isolated fragments have survived. The scenario published here not only reverses the usual script/film order, but is separated from the cinematic work by an interval of some twenty years. Dovzhenko himself described it as 'a kind of literary equivalent' of the ideas he had put into his film.

Reference to the surviving fragments of the shooting script, and of course to the film itself, show that the basic narrative line has been adhered to — where omissions or additions occur, these have been footnoted.

What chiefly distinguishes this version is the introduction of a narrator through whom events and characters are personalised; this is particularly strongly felt in the introductory passage centring on the death of grandfather Semyon. The interest of this innovation in relation to the film lies in the fact that the narrator is both film-maker and spectator at once, and therefore opens the way for comment on the choices which brought certain images to the screen and reflections on their form. Implicitly too, there is an element of hindsight in the narrator's stress on the film's 'muteness' and its implications for the film-maker, actors and spectator; the intervening years had seen a major transformation in cinematic techniques and the effects of sound on the art of scenario writing was a question which prompted one of Dovzhenko's relatively rare excursions into theoretical writing.

Originally written in Ukranian, this version was completed by Dovzhenko four years before his death in 1956.

Diana Matias

EARTH

Did it really happen, or was it a dream? Have dreams merged into memories, and memories of memories — I'm no longer sure. I only remember that Grandfather was very old. And I remember that he used to look like one of the images on the icons that graced and guarded our old house.

Whenever I looked in the garden — among the apple trees and pear trees, currant bushes and gooseberries — I could be sure to catch the gleam of his saintly white beard.

I remember too that it was a sultry summer's day and everything around me was beautiful — the orchard, the vegetable patch, the sunflowers and poppies, and the ripening cornfields beyond the orchard. And my grandfather Semyon, the one-time oxcart driver, was lying under the apple tree that grew not far from our cellar in the orchard. Lying there among the fallen apples on an ancient white bench, dressed in his white peasant shirt, he looked all white and transparent from age and goodness.

He was a hundred years old. Actually, he was probably something less, but somehow I like to think of him as precisely a hundred — there's something fine in that. And the way he lay there, like a figure in a painting, was beautiful too. He even seemed to glow a little. At least it seemed that way to me because it was Sunday, and some other kind of holiday as well. On an old apple tree stump next to my grandfather sat his old friend and companion, Petro. He was also very old, but he didn't have a beard and so he lacked Grandfather's patriarchal appearance. Instead of a beard he wore a ferocious, tobacco-stained moustache which made him look rather like an ancient warrior. Grandfather used to tell us that once, a long time ago, Petro had been the strongest man in the whole province. They had travelled the steppes with their oxcarts full of salt and alcohol, from Chernigov and Konotop to Stavropol, Berdyansk and Jasi, even to Moscow itself, and nowhere had they met anyone who was a match for him. He was a withdrawn and taciturn man, but he really loved Grandfather and visited him at least twice a year. He used to dress neatly, move slowly, and always seemed lost in thought.

On this occasion too he sat with his friend in silence, only after a time asking: ' Are you dying, Semyon? '

' Yes Petro, I'm dying,' Grandfather admitted quietly and smiling a little closed his eyes.

Mother came up just then and when she saw what was happening in the orchard she grew very thoughtful.

' Well, so be it then,' Petro said and turned away.

One of the children, a baby still quite innocent of life, was sitting on the grass among the fallen apples. His mouth wide open, he was trying with all his might to bite into an apple with his two first teeth, but the apple was big and his child's mouth wasn't big enough yet.

' So be it then Semyon,' said Petro. ' But when you go, send me a sign from over there — let me know if you're in heaven or hell, and how things are with you.'

' I will, Petro,' promised Grandfather as he gathered himself up for his final journey. ' If it can be done, I'll let you know, you can be sure of that. You'll see me in one of your dreams, or in a vision maybe . . .' Affectionately, he discussed the simple possibilities of future meetings with his friend.

But since Grandfather wasn't dying of any illness, he didn't die immediately. On the contrary, he still managed to sit up slowly unaided and looked around at all of us. (*Still*) His son Opanas and grandchildren Vasil and Orisya came down from the house carrying a beautiful bowl of pears.

' It might be nice to eat something,' grandfather mused, looking around at his family, and when Orisya brought him the bowl of pears he took one and wiped it slowly on the sleeve of his white shirt. It was his favourite ruddy kind, but it was obvious that Grandfather had eaten his fill of pears. He just munched halfheartedly, from habit more than anything. At that moment his heart must have started to slow down and he sensed it. Laying the pear to one side he arranged his beard and shirt, looked around at us all once more, and folding his arms on his chest he said with a smile: ' Well goodbye, I'm dying.' Then he slowly lay back and died.

' He used to love pears.' Orisya's elder brother Vasil turned to her with a sad, thoughtful smile, then looked back at his grandfather again. All his obligations fulfilled, our ancestor lay under the apple tree in his white shirt, and the calloused hands crossed on his chest bore witness.

It's here I think that the film begins, though generally speaking nothing very special happened after this either. Grandfather's death provoked no upheaval in the surrounding universe — there was no clap of thunder, no lightning rent the sky, no storm uprooted the venerable oaks.

Instead, the midday sky was cloudless. Everything was perfectly still — two or three apples thudded into the grass somewhere nearby, and that was all. Not even a sunflower stirred — that whole bright world of sunflowers was motionless, standing like a choir of beautiful children with their happy, golden-brown faces turned to the sky. (*Still*) And the golden bees that Grandfather had now abandoned darted over the lime trees in silence. Nor did anything out of the ordinary happen to Grandfather's kinsfolk. It had all come about so naturally that those closest to him could contemplate him now without feeling any overwhelming grief or pain. The emotion that came over them gradually was a strange, solemn sense of the mystery of existence, as if they had all been unexpectedly touched by eternity and its harmonious laws. And even in death Grandfather hadn't relinquished his smile — it went on softly illuminating his face. His features had never been of a heroic kind.

It's quite possible that we won't be able to express all this satisfactorily in our film and it probably isn't really necessary that we should. I have written it down more to honour custom and my kinsfolk, and in part too for the enlightenment of the actors.

The actor who represents the humble person of my grandfather must nevertheless have a number of personal qualities — without them no amount of histrionics will enable him to preserve that smile after death. As the actors have probably already guessed, Grandfather was a simple, uneducated man, a fact which did not prevent him and Petro from playing a notable role in the education and enlightenment of the Ukranian people in the nineteenth century. For some third of a century their oxcarts carried books from Moscow to Kharkov University along the Black Sea highway. They often used to reminisce about it over their vodka in the garden.

'Ah! If it hadn't been for Petro and me, no one would have got so much as a whiff of learning in Kharkov. How many books we brought in those thirty years! You could have made a thousand pairs of shoes from the bindings.'

'You're right,' his companion would reply. 'I wonder who's reading them today? Anyone that's read the lot must be sharper than the devil himself.'

The actor must be neither very tall nor very short. He must be broad-shouldered, grey-eyed, with a high, clear forehead and that smile that it's so pleasant to remember now. He must know how to handle a scythe, a pitchfork and a lathe, how to build a cottage or make a good cart without the smallest scrap of metal, and how to do all sorts of useful things quickly and cheerfully. He must have no fear of rain or snow, or distant journeys, or the weight of a load on his back. If he were called to war, he wouldn't lag behind in a charge or counter-attack, he would't shirk reconnaissance duty, and he'd know how to go without food for two or three days and still keep his spirits up. If a trench needed digging, he'd be there, and he'd be ready to give a hand when the guns or someone else's vehicle had to be dragged out of the mud. He'd know how to talk kindly — not just to simple people and those in command, but to horses and calves, to the sun in the sky and the grass on the ground. If he qualified in all this he would be the very image of my grandfather. But if we're not lucky enough to find such an actor at a reasonable price and we have to make do instead with some miserable drunkard or a boaster upgraded by some lucky chance and immediately turned arrogant, the kind of actor for whom the world exists only insofar as it revolves around his person — then don't lay the blame on the deceased. The guilt will lie with art.

Yes, I would say this gives a fair picture of a particular event in my personal life — the death of my grandfather in the summer of 1930 under the apple tree in the small orchard he himself had neatly fenced off.

And if all this really can't be suitably adapted to our future film, then we might best begin the first part with a song:

Out of the skies
Tumbles the clear dawn . . .

Is there any other country where they sing so resonantly, freely and beautifully as they do in the Ukraine? I write this not at all out of a desire to present my people to the world in an exaggerated and favourable light, but in the interests of realism, and I'm sure all lovers of good singing agree without reservation. I used to come home from work with Vasil, the hero of my film, accompanied by just this song. What can be sweeter and more cheering than work well done? What can be pleasanter after a hard day's mowing in the cheerful meadow than walking home into the sunset? The body aches pleasantly, there is peace in your heart, you're nineteen years old and you feel ' her ' presence somewhere near you, and you both feel the warm earth under your bare feet, beaten down by wheels and hooves, covered with warm, feathery dust or wonderfully gentle mud that tickles your toes. The words just sing themselves:

Stroll on, be merry, young maid,
I will see you home . . .

A warm sense of comradeship accompanies you as you walk, and you see the evening sky, the bright sunset glow, and ' her ' with her pitchfork over her round, girlish shoulder.

But let's not complicate the plot with introductory scenes, however close they may be to the heart; let's just follow the events since they have already begun.

Lightning streaked the sky beyond Grandfather's fence. A storm was uprooting the venerable oaks and thunder shattered the stillness. The sounds of weeping and confusion filled the air. It was Arkhip Belokon — tearing his shirt and clasping his hoary head in his hands. Despair was choking Belokon — he was gripped by a hatred so intense that it seemed to make his very house tremble.

The women of the house — his wife and two daughters and the grandmother — were all lamenting. The dogs were howling. Even the horses sensed disaster and stamped and snorted in the stable.

67

Who was the object of the curses Belokon hurled as he gnashed his teeth in the window? And what were his two neighbours — his brothers — and the aged Father Gerasim doing in his house? What was the cause of such terrible fear? What had happened?

The village had existed in this way for centuries, nestling under the mountain beside a sleepy backwater, its people working, bearing children, loving, ploughing, sowing, harvesting, singing, laughing, crying, and dying, as peacefully as at the bottom of a lake. So when something did happen, it was always something unheard of and undreamed of anywhere else in the world. What was it, where did it come from, why and how? There would be endless discussion in the days following, eyewitness accounts many times re-told would merge with other recollections and with the tales of the old yarn-spinners of the village until it was impossible to tell whether things had happened that way or not, or even whether they had happened at all. And so, had Belokon dreamt all this? No, this was no dream. It had really happened. The Revolution had given rise to a new order as surely as light produces light. The Socialist Revolution had brought the banner of collectivisation to the countryside.

But Arkhip Belokon refused to see, and this malevolent and benighted landowner would go on refusing to understand until such time as he was transported far away, until his voice was heard no more, and no trace of the kulak breed remained on the land.

So it was not for nothing that the dogs were howling in the courtyard. The time had come for the accounts of all centuries past to be settled on the land, in accordance with the principles of Marx.

Arkhip Belokon was desperate. Had he not laboured hard? His throat was dry with hatred. For the hundredth time that day he cursed the authorities, the harvest and the land, and even the rain which he had called on to leave the kolkhoz fields unwatered.

If only he could have got his hands on Vasil — the village's collective farm representative. Even if the soul had left his body and he had lain a lifeless corpse in the middle of the courtyard, bewailed by his entire family, even dead, Belokon would still have shuddered with hatred.

' Leave off your whining, you lot! '

His fist struck the table sending the bread and knife leaping into the air. The silence that followed was the sort that precedes an explosion.

' Read on, Father,' Belokon groaned, fixing his morose, staring eyes on the paper in Father Gerasim's hands.

Father Gerasim read out what was virtually a funeral oration for all enemies of the new collective farm life, and for Belokon in particular: '. . . Arkhip Belokon, is undermining the collective system, hiding grain, slaughtering live-stock . . .'

Again the women set up their wailing, in four different keys. Belokon covered his face with his hands. Then in desperation he grabbed an axe and rushed into the passageway. His family rushed after him. Where was he going? He didn't know himself. He thought he was rushing out to slaughter Vasil, who at that moment was standing by the body of his dead grandfather. Belokon imagined himself white-lipped, rushing up to Vasil and grabbing him by the throat. As he prepared to swing the axe, his wife and daughter seized his arm and held him back.

' Let go! '

But they clung on and the youngest Belokon also came running to restrain his father. For it wasn't Vasil that Belokon held — it was his own horse in his own stable.

' Let me go, I'll kill him! '

The other horses stirred nervously.

Vasil's father Opanas Trubenko was a peasant of average means and by nature a slow man. He had never hurried anywhere in his life and remained true to himself to this day. He was in no rush to join the collective although he had long ago made up his mind. It seemed to him that there were nevertheless still a number of reasons for not joining. First one thing, then another cropped up, and now old Grandfather's death . . . He'd even more or less joined on one or two occasions, but then he'd dropped out again — they hadn't written his name down properly, or something like that. Besides, who could tell? Perhaps it wouldn't work out right. It was a difficult problem.

69

' I don't know myself what's best,' he once admitted to his wife Odarka, when the children weren't about. ' They've got every reason to call us middle-of-the-road peasants — here am I with one of my ears listening to the farm board and to Vasil, and the other to my own voice whispering — "don't do it, don't do it ".'
' You're right,' sighed his wife.
' The world has changed. Wherever my eyes look, wherever I turn, I sense it. Even our old house isn't the same any more. Have you noticed? It's as if it didn't altogether belong to us any more, though it does of course. As if cracks had appeared in the walls and the roof had blown off and everything was open to view ... open to view and insecure. But you can't make the Dniepr flow backwards, Odarka, and it's the same with life. You can't bring back the past.'
Opanas fell silent. His wife looked at him in astonishment. She'd never known him to say so much ... After a moment's thought Opanas sighed: ' Perhaps we should join, what do you think? The collective I mean. Vasil would be pleased ... You know how it is, people are saying — " He's the collective's representative, goes round talking other people into it, but his mother and father stay away." '
' Well, all right,' said Odarka, but the next thing she said implicitly withdrew the consent she seemed to be giving. ' We'll do it if that's how you feel. But I say one thing — we'll join, but the oxen and the cows stay where they are.'
Opanas said nothing. He knew from simple experience that apart from a bit of extra noise, there was nothing to be gained from contradicting his wife. In any case, he was a kind and gentle man and he didn't want to upset his partner. They were expecting another child in a few days.
Vasil was overjoyed. His father's decision to join the collective seemed to give him wings. True, his mother's naive ' conditions ' still had to be overcome, but all in all it was good and sensible. In a little while, they too would see that it was good and sensible. The day before at the kolkhoz headquarters he'd been shown a map of the collective farm fields and his lively imagination had transformed those plans into a purposeful project of his own life, leading even to fame perhaps. He saw himself as no longer just a simple village activist, but as Vasil

Trubenko — statesman.

'We can ring the death knell for the kulaks now,' he told his father. 'We'll get machines. All we need is machines.'

Opanas Trubenko knew something about machines. In his early youth he had worked for Pfalzfein in Kakhovka for a few years and he'd seen a machine harvesting the crop. But why should all this be up to Vasil? Why did it have to be his job? Let someone else do a bit — there was no lack of good men in the village. But Vasil was already standing before his father ready for the journey. Opanas drummed his fingers on the table.

'Vasil, maybe it's not you . . . What I mean is . . .'

Vasil didn't understand his father's concern, he hardly seemed to hear him. He was caught up in his own joy and readiness for action.

'If we get the machine, we'll take all the kulaks' land. All of it.'

Opanas looked out of the window, chewing on a crust of bread.

'That's what I mean, maybe it's not . . . What I mean is . . . perhaps they can do without you.'

Vasil shook his head and even burst out laughing. Opanas was offended — how did he dare to mock his parents at his age!

'You don't have to go. As it is the whole village is laughing.'

'But it's not the whole village,' Vasil said, 'It's the kulaks, and the fools.'

'So that's it. That's how you speak to your parents these days.' Opanas even got up from the table. 'So in your opinion I'm a fool.'

'No, I didn't mean that, Father, only that you've got old.' Vasil looked straight at his father and smiled.

Nobody knows what Opanas would have said to that for the door suddenly opened to admit Vasil's new friend, the secretary of the local Komsomol, Chuprina or Kravchina, Opanas could never remember his name. He just nicknamed him the Cell. It wasn't that he disliked him. Possibly he even liked him, but at a distance. In the house and at close range, he couldn't bear more than half an hour of his company because Chuprina — or was it Kravchina? — depressed him so much with all his noise, laughter and incredibly loud and rapid talk.

'Aha, the Cell's here.' Opanas turned his back and sat down at the table. 'Well, you can start the meeting.'

71

Before giving the speaker the floor, we must be fair: Opanas actually liked this Chuprina, or Kravchina, even at close range. It wasn't important that his mouth stretched from ear to ear or that his face was smothered in freckles — his ideas were good, and he produced so many one after another. The one thing that Opanas found hard to take was that he was always lecturing. He wasn't at all embarrassed by his own youth or another's age — he just lectured everyone, whoever happened to turn up. Teaching was like drawing breath to him. As for tact — don't even ask. He had no rank and very likely he wasn't even old enough for military service.

' I won't turn around,' Opanas muttered frowning, 'let him talk now that he's here.'

What exactly Kravchina, or Chuprina, talked to Opanas about we unfortunately cannot convey, for all our cinematographic skills. It had to be heard — that was the whole point.

Here, all we can see is that Kravchina's mouth is never shut, his eyes give off sparks, he seems to have a hundred teeth, and his freckles dance furiously over his face. All we can see is that he throws his whole agile frame, his unruly red hair, his merry smile, and his rich range of expressions into the task of talking sense into Opanas, treating him like a recalcitrant child, alternately mocking, cajoling, reproaching and admonishing. The whole image radiates irrepressible, dynamic youth and an optimism which excludes all possibility of doubt. The whole house is enlivened by his presence so that when Kravchina-Chuprina finally leaves with Vasil, slamming the door behind him, and still loudly continuing the conversation in the passageway, through the yard and into the street, Opanas turns around and says bemusedly: ' Well, I'll be damned! ' He even gets to his feet to look out of the window.

Opanas couldn't get that conversation out of his head for a long time. ' They could be right of course. They probably are. Times have changed. You won't get far with oxen these days, sweat though you may over your own poor strip,' he mused to himself.

Suddenly Vasil's voice was heard from the street: ' I'm going, father.'

Opanas looked out and there was Vasil, accompanied by others

72

like him and of course with Kravchina at the head. They all carried bundles on sticks over their shoulders — and they were off to the town to get a tractor. How beautifully they sang. No worse than Opanas had in his day, and maybe even better.

Opanas watched them go until they were lost in a dip in the road and only their song was heard: 'Stroll on, be merry, young maid, I will see you home . . .' while the long straight line of telegraph poles could be seen stretching endlessly into the distance.

Meanwhile, old man Petro had smeared his head with olive oil from the icon lamp and was making his way to the cemetery to visit his old friend. Once the cemetery used to be outside the village. But gradually both the dead and the living had extended their territory until now the cemetery was almost in the village itself. There was more than one advantage in this situation. While you couldn't really say that the dead felt more at home there since the dead don't feel anything any more, you could say without fear of contradiction that they were closer to home. The children of the village played among their graves, the old women spent their Sundays there. The old people used to say that even dying was less terrifying in our village. Nothing special like granite or marble monuments marked the graves. Linen and crockery was put out to dry among the crosses, which were quite simple wooden ones. Grandfather Semyon had one of these plain crosses freshly made from ash tree wood. That must have pleased him since he'd never been fond of iron when he was alive. It was at this cross that Petro stopped.

Although we have already said that Petro was a man of few words, we want to stress the point here. It became doubly noticeable after his unsuccessful journey to the Far East in 1907.[1]

Petro loved peace. When he heard that somewhere along the Pacific Ocean there was free land, he recalled his early years of travel to faraway places and didn't waste much time pondering the matter. He just harnessed his piebald mare and set out silently 'under his own steam' for the East. He was accom-

---

[1] The following interlude relating to Petro's journey to the Far East and his return does not appear in the film.

panied by his wife Kharitina and his dog Sultan, whom he deeply respected for his discretion and his aversion to barking . . . Sultan carried out all his duties in silence . . .

Petro got together a great quantity of all sorts of provisions for the journey, especially tobacco. But more especially he equipped himself with patience, the necessity for which had nothing at all to do with the length of the journey, although it measured half the world's equator.

To make the picture quite clear we should also say that while the mare, Sultan and old man Petro were all dedicated to peace and respected silence, Kharitina on the other hand liked to voice her feelings and desires loudly whatever the cause. And as her desires were in the main directed at Petro, the mare or Sultan, then it has to be said at once that if even a one-thousandth part of her wishes had been translated into action — neither Petro nor the mare, nor Sultan would have seen the bright shores of the Pacific Ocean. They would have long ago dropped by the roadside from the plague, cholera, or various other ills wished on them by Kharitina, and what's more not one of them would have been granted rest in the bosom of Mother Earth.

It would be a fairly simple matter to make a separate two-part film of Petro's journey to the Pacific Ocean in search of peace and back again. But to avoid confusion we had best make the most of this beautiful summer morning and move straight to the remote little provincial town from which he set out on his travels.

What's all the commotion in the market place about? Where are all the market people hurrying so eagerly? Has old Petro, the one they call Tovchenik, returned from the Far East? That's it, you've guessed it.

Arriving in the market place after such a long absence, old man Petro of course attracted everyone's attention. Before half an hour was up he had the whole market place buzzing around him like bees around their queen bee.

' Old Petro's back! '

' Where from? Which one? "

' The one they call Tovchenik! From Green Lea! '

' From Green Lea, you say. Is Kharitina with him? '

' Kharitina too, there she is.'

74

'Kharitina, and the mare, and Sultan?'
'The very same.'
'Hello, Petro.'
'Hello.'
And in fact the mare, and Sultan the dog were just about the same as they had been before Petro's departure from Green Lea. And having travelled over various geographical latitudes for a distance of some twenty thousand kilometres, the mare and Sultan came to a halt on the very same square from which they had begun their journey to the Pacific Ocean three and a half years earlier.
'How many versts is that?' Grandfather Semyon, who was still alive then, asked Petro.
'Who bothered to count?' replied the traveller reticently. 'Nobody does.'
'They say it's twenty thousand each way.'
'Who knows? Could be as many as that I reckon.'
'So why did you come back from such a distance?' asked the neighbours.
'The wife didn't like it.'
At this the entire market place collapsed in helpless laughter. Their unrestrained mirth terrified Sultan, who leaped under the cart and proceeded to revile the crowd with his angry barking. Even the piebald raised its head and backed in the shafts. Only Petro remained unperturbed. He just adjusted the harness on his round-the-world steed with the end of his Siberian whip and patiently waited for the laughter to subside. He seemed to want to say something more on the subject of his wife, who sat behind him all this time like a broody goose, but at this point the director of the local folklore museum, a learned and inquisitive man, intervened: 'You know, Petro Tarasevich, your horse should be skinned immediately, stuffed with straw and set up in the museum. It's a phenomenon.'
'All right by me,' said Petro, taking out his tobacco pouch, 'only it's not the horse I'd have skinned, but somebody else, and who that is exactly I'll tell you when I'm dying.'
'Help me good people!' Kharitina suddenly burst into life. 'He's ready to kill me — may God strike him down. Holy Mother of God!'

'That's what it was like all the way,' Petro said with a wave of the hand, and fell silent. Abandoning all hope of peace, he began to think more about the heavenly kind. After the death of his friend Semyon, he stopped talking altogether.

Petro arrived at Semyon's grave. Dropping to his knees and looking around to see if anyone noticed, Petro bent his head and laid an ear to the grave. He listened for a long time, holding his breath in case he should get a sign from his friend. But no sign came so he asked insistently, keeping his voice low:
'Semyon, where are you?' (*Still*)
Just then to his chagrin he was unpleasantly interrupted. A pair of six-year-old ruffians — how the earth supports their like is a mystery — popped up from behind a neighbouring grave and shouted in chorus: 'Hello Grandad!'
Petro fell silent and, frowning fiercely, bent back to the grave. The boys hid. Petro looked around and there was no one in sight. 'What was that all about? Am I hearing things or was it some kind of sign?'
'Semyon, answer me. Where are you?' he asked again, bending right down to the ground, but no answer came.
'Hello, Grandad!' The two childish voices rang out again from behind a clump of guelder rose on the next grave. Those urchins again. Petro raised his head.
'Hello!' shrilled one of them a third time and quickly ducked behind the bush.
'Get away and stop teasing me! Off, devil take you! Let me have some peace!'
Petro lost his temper and went home. He didn't once look back and he didn't see that one of the boys' eyes had filled with tears and he'd run home in childish distress.

There's a picturesque knoll on the outskirts of the village where a wide view opens out onto the other side of the river and the steppes. On Sunday, after the midday meal, a crowd of people had gathered around the now armless windmill.[1]

---

[1] In this section, as elsewhere, the action in the film is interspersed with purely 'pictorial' shots of animals, people, etc., which have no direct equivalent in the scenario. A number of these are included in the illustrations, but only those which can be directly related to the action are given reference in the text.

It was a glorious day. The girls' white dresses sparkled against the blue sky, some of them embroidered with such faultless taste that they might have aroused the envy of a princess, if any such still exist in the wilds of Europe. The young men were also dressed with special care. Khoma Belokon's shirtfront was a profusion of embroidery, a regular vegetable garden. A cap of the old-fashioned kind with the tight band sat precariously on his bristly head. Beside him stood Ustim Reva, head raised and thick-lipped mouth open to catch the sunflower seeds he was skilfully tossing in the air. (*Still*)

Everyone's eyes were turned in the direction of the field. A rumour had been heard, apparently emanating from the station 28 kilometres away, that a tractor was on its way to the village under its own steam, and that after this neither horses nor boundary marks would be needed in the fields — tractors didn't like boundaries it seemed — and everything would be different. Could this be so? Never!

Old Ulas Reva, round-bellied and grey as an ox himself, stood motionless on top of the Scythian grave with his two oxen, looking out to the steppe like a statue out of another age. (*Still*) The first to spot the tractor in the field was Opanas' youngest son, the seventeen-year-old Andreyko. He was perched on a tall fence when he first caught sight of a cloud of dust on the steppes far away on the horizon, and he let out a joyful yell: ' They're coming! '

' They're coming! They're coming! ' The other boys took up his cry in a chorus, and leaping down from fences and thatched roofs, they raced into the fields beating up clouds of dust with their bare feet as they energetically whipped up their imaginary steeds. The adults also surged forward in a mass.

Khoma Belokon and Reva ran up onto the Scythian mound, craning their long necks and even opening their mouths as they listened for the sound of the machine. Vasil's father Opanas Trubenko was also staring intently into the distance. Was it a tractor or not? There had been another such occasion, back in the time of the Tsar, when everyone had gathered at this same place to meet the Archbishop who was to bless the church. The dust had whirled over the steppes just like this and curiosity had overwhelmed people, just like this. But it had turned out to be no Archbishop, just a drunken Grigory Sirik whipping his master's horses across the fields, which is why ever after that the nickname Archbishop stuck to him. Even the Revolution hadn't changed that. Now it wasn't simply that the neighbours had forgotten his surname; Sirik himself calmly referred to himself as Archbishop and to his children as the 'little Archbishops'.

This time it was the tractor and no mistake. Brand new, full of bounce, and driven by Vasil. How many horsepower it had even Vasil didn't know, and neither did any of his friends. But judging from the way they rolled swiftly and joyfully towards their native village, from the sweat streaming down their faces and backs, and the smiles that flashed on their suntanned faces, what propelled the tractor was not horsepower but some other kind of power which had not yet been given a name. This was the first tractor — a revolutionary on the wide fields of the Ukraine.

But suddenly the worst happened. The 'revolutionary' spluttered, panted, let out a cloud of steam from its radiator, and stopped . . .

Cameramen, quick! Sling your cameras over your shoulders and at the double into the fields! The tractor mustn't stop under the eyes of the people.

A telephone call had already come through from town asking if the tractor had arrived. 'Yes,' they'd been told, 'it's arrived, in perfect shape and met by a huge crowd.'

What was to be done? Vasil had long ago noticed that there seemed to be no cap on the radiator, but he'd thought perhaps that was how it was supposed to be — then again, perhaps not, who knew? He was embarrassed — he was the one who'd been shown how to handle the tractor. He thought he might have left it behind somewhere. 'Well, never mind,' he thought, 'we'll get there all right this time — it's not far.' But when the remains of the water in the radiator boiled over and a column of hot steam rushed out of the opening, Vasil stopped the machine.

'Vasil, why are you stopping?' his friends asked anxiously, also sensing disaster.

'Well say something, people are watching. Lord, what a mess!

Look, here they come running! '
' The cap's lost,' said Vasil not trying to conceal his desperation.
' It should be here, see. Where it's got to, the devil knows. We must have forgotten it back at the pumping station, or some son of a bitch has unscrewed it deliberately. What are we going to do? The arrival's going to be a disaster.' (*Still*) Komsomol leader Chuprina was helpless with rage. He sat down in the roadway and started banging his stave against the ground furiously, as if he were thrashing an imaginary culprit. Meanwhile, the far from imaginary culprit stood alongside experiencing the incident in his own way. Ivan Khakalo was so ashamed of himself he wished the ground could swallow him up. In a few years time he was to become a famous tractor driver. His pictures would be in the Moscow papers, journalists would print his life story. A gold star would decorate his honourable broad chest; all things are possible in this world. But as long as he lived, labour hero Ivan Khakalo would never forget this dark page of his glorious biography, try though he may to skip over it or omit it altogether. He took the radiator cap out of his pocket, fumbled with it for a moment in embarrassment, then held it out nervously to Vasil.

' Maybe you could screw this on? '

' That's it! ' yelled Vasil.

' What? '

' The cap. Where'd you get it? '

' But this isn't a cap — it's metal.'

' Metal yourself — you idiot! '

' Well, let's not fight about it now.' Khakalo was in an agony of remorse. ' Look, Vasil — Don't get mad. Listen, I just thought — it's a hot day and, well, it'll cool the water.'

' What are you talking about you clown! ' shrieked Chuprina in such a fury that the freckles on his face seemed to triple in number. ' We'll talk about this cap at the Komsomol meeting and you'll be dropped for six months. How are we supposed to build socialism with idiots like you! '

' We will! Don't yell at me, what are you shouting for? ' Khakalo was offended. ' Don't you think I feel bad enough — I don't need any help from you to make me ashamed of my ignorance.'

' Well, O.K. Where are we going to get the water from now? The engine will melt at the seams without water. Look, the kids are nearly here.'

They were all in despair. Then Khakalo's mind cleared. Let the Chamberlains and Wellses over there in London split their sides at the film maker and his heroes. It was our affair, after all. The important thing was not to give the kulaks, the Belokons, something to laugh at. And no doubt they were already up there on the mound, on the alert, sharpening their miserable, sarcastic wits.

We won't look too deeply into the details, because facts alone can always appear to be one thing or another, depending on the intention behind them. When victory hangs in the balance at the front and with it the destiny of your people, when the machine-gun casing gets red hot and there's no water about, and the enemy keeps pressing, it isn't important where the gunners get the water — every second is precious then and every movement of the body is magnificent. The tractor is ours! [1] (*Still*)

' Ready? '

' Ready.'

' Screw the cap on and let's go! (*Still*)

Joy broke out. They were on the threshold of triumph. The boys were already on top of them and their fathers were no less excited. The whole procession moved off and at the outskirts of the village the people surged forward to meet them. Surrounded by an excited hubbub of voices, Vasil and his friends stopped the tractor in the village square.

Arkhip Belokon, who had watched the procession from his window, turned ashen with despair.

' Everything's lost. This is the end.' His legs seemed about to give under him. Turning his shaggy head to look at Father Gerasim he said in a strangled voice: ' We're finished.'

People converged on the machine from all sides. They had soon wiped the dust from the ploughshares and read the trade mark.

' We have here an authentic, concrete engine — it's a fact,' one

---

[1] As the accompanying still suggests, the problem is solved by the workers urinating into the tractor's radiator. However, this sequence was apparently cut by the Russian censor and does not now appear in the film.

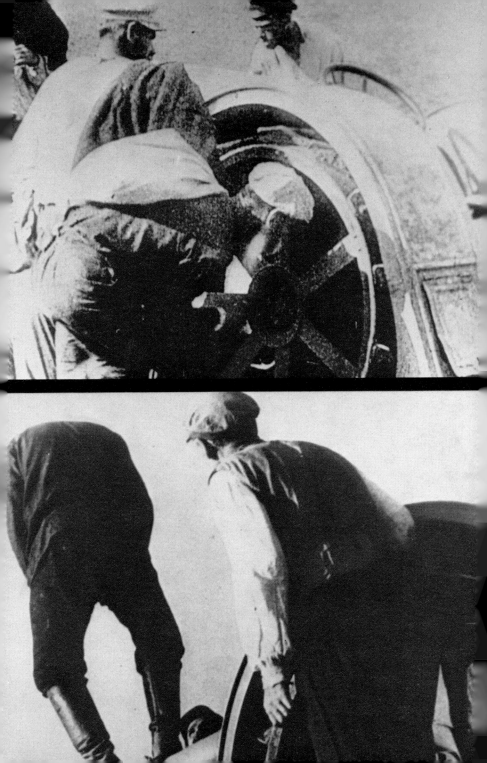

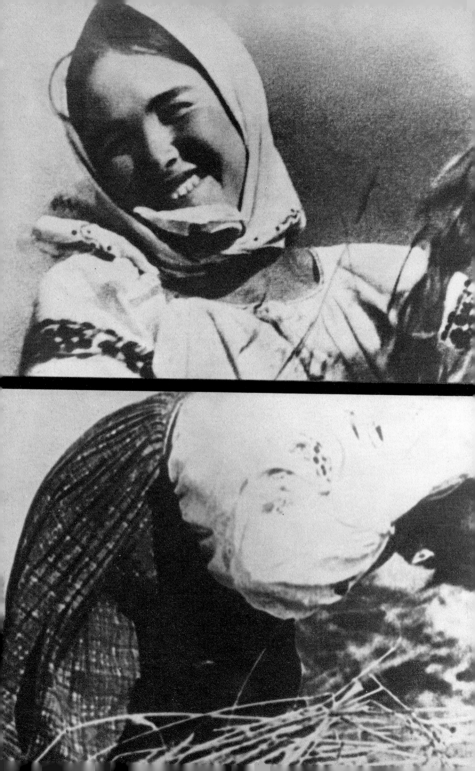

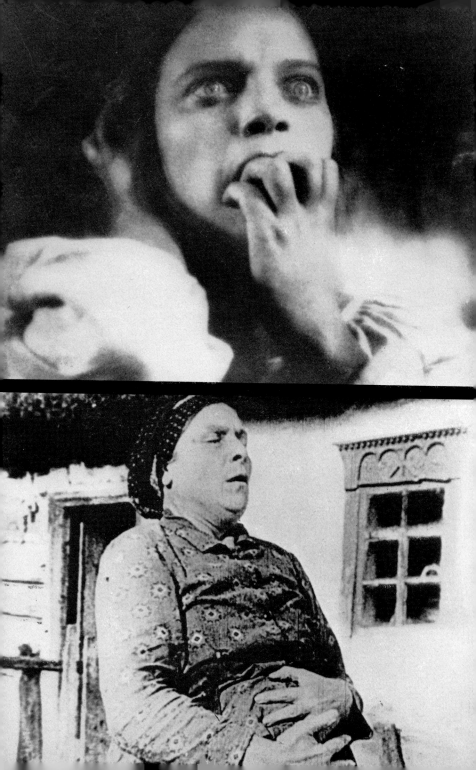

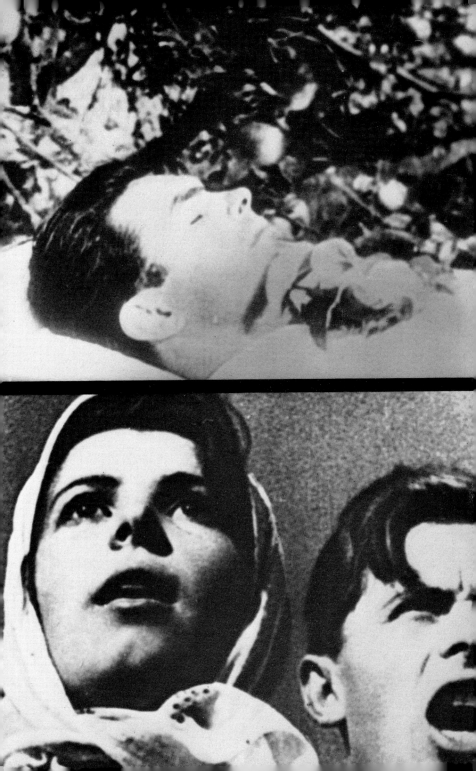

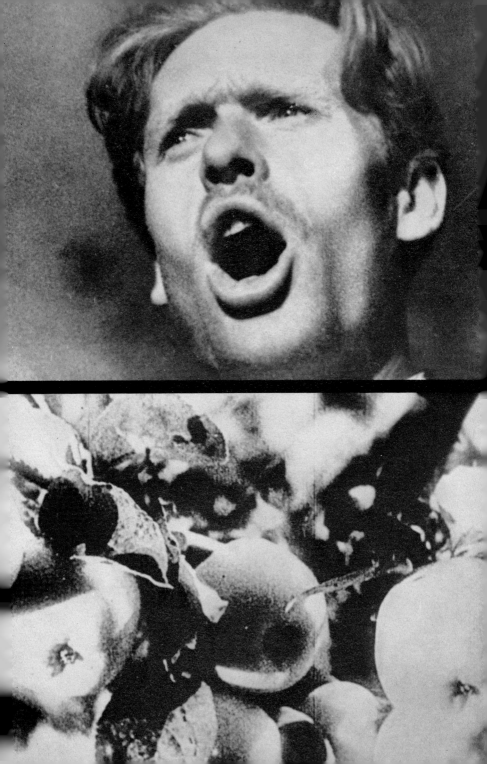

of the senior activists of the kolkhoz with a weakness for intellectual jargon announced loudly. He was Kuprin Soroka, nicknamed Governor. This elegant title had been bestowed on him by his fellow citizens some forty years earlier when quite unexpectedly he'd been summoned to the district court over some land affair. He'd galloped off unshaven before daybreak and got to Chernigov and back before evening, having covered over 150 kilometres — or versts, as they used to be called.

' Well, what was that all about? ' asked the neighbours.

' A mistake. The wrong surname, they said. And there was me wondering all the way what the devil that fool governor wanted with me.'

Governor tapped the tractor's ploughshares with the whip he held and again voiced his fullest appreciation of the importance of the event, casting a stern glance at the onlookers.

Vasil was happy. Taking off his cap he wiped his damp forehead and listened to the excited hum of voices all around him.

' May the tractor serve you well,' he said cheerfully, addressing himself to the crowd. ' Grandad Governor here has made a true observation. This is an accomplished " fact ".' Vasil slapped the hot metal with the palm of his hand. 'Now everything is going to be different. Now we can definitely say — the last days have come for the boundary marks and for the kulak fields.' (Still)

' Watch out it's not the last days of someone your mother'd miss,' a voice called roughly from over near the kulak houses. It was Khoma. (Still) Some hundred people stood between Vasil and Khoma and as Vasil turned they fell back to clear a path for him. Vasil got down from the tractor and slowly walked up to his enemy, still smiling.

Khoma was a bit drunk, or perhaps he was suffering the effects of all the excitement. An unruly clump of hair stuck out aggressively from under the cap that shaded his glazed eyes, and the shell of a sunflower seed clung to his damp lower lip. The kulak lad was so big that Vasil looked like a boy beside him.

' Say that again,' said Vasil, surveying Khoma calmly. His voice was unruffled.

' I've said what I wanted to say,' Khoma retorted, still aggressively, but a little less sure of himself.

' All right then, we'll see . . .'

' That's right, we'll see . . .'

' Vasil — why waste your words on him, why bother with a fool? ' Governor intervened. He looked at Khoma scornfully — ' It's like talking to a bull. Siberia's where he belongs, mark my words.'

Laughter broke out around them. Some of the colour left Khoma's face and he made an arrogant show of clearing his throat.

Ustim Reva glanced apprehensively at his friend. Perhaps he knew something, or guessed. Whatever it was, an animal fear flickered in those round black eyes.

A few days later was some minor church feast day which more than half the village had ceased to observe since the Revolution. In the afternoon Khoma, with the chapel master in tow, went round the village completely drunk, stamping his shiny boots and shouting at the top of his voice:

' Come on! — I'll pay you to throw me! '

Suddenly Ustim appeared from round a corner.

' Khoma! ' he shouted, breathless from a long, breakneck run. ' Hey! Khoma! Vasil's ploughed down the boundaries with the tractor! '

Khoma froze. For three days he said not a word to anyone. The rest of the enemies of the collective said nothing either. Only the bulls bellowed from time to time at night and the smell of home-brewed vodka wafted out of the richer kulak houses. But they say you could hear the gnashing of teeth.

The tractor achieved unheard of marvels in the fields. When it made its first furrow it was followed not just by the village children, but the adults too, and the members of the collective farm board. But when Vasil went on to plough all the plots in just a few days, turning the separate patches of land into one unbounded, velvety field, people stopped: some of them looked on in delight, others in silent wonder, still others became profoundly thoughtful . . . People sensed many great things happening within themselves and in this new world.[1]

---

[1] In the film, the ploughing is preceded by a montage sequence in which Vasil reaps the corn with the help of the tractor, the women gather it into sheaves, and it is threshed, milled and made into bread. Two stills from this sequence are included in the illustrations.

'Well Opanas, what do you say?' Grandad Governor asked Opanas, who was ploughing his own poor strip. 'See what your Vasil has done?'

'I'll say one thing,' Opanas stopped his plough. 'There's going to be a hundred times less horses in this village, people like us are going to have to do some thinking. The work-horse's life is finished.'

When Vasil with his happy smile steered the tractor over his own grandfather's boundaries and nodded cheerily to his father, shouting something as he passed, Opanas stopped and looked after his son for a long time.

For the first time in his life he felt himself to be small and helpless. And he saw the life he had lived as perhaps wretched and miserable, not the life he should have lived. He felt a profound urge to follow after his son, to retrieve the irretrievable. 'How many years have I crawled over this plot of mine with my horses, soaked in my own sweat!'

Evening came. The radiant July day slowly faded. Its sunset glowed in the sky. And then the gentle Ukranian night closed in.

The moon poured its soft light over the world, lending an air of enchantment to the couples on benches and tree stumps around the white-washed houses. This was where the shy girls met their chosen sweethearts in the evenings, and sat breathless and still under touches that trembled on the brink of forbidden spheres; cheek to warm cheek they sat, watching wide-eyed the glittering night sky. (*Still*)

Men slept with their arms flung wide, in houses, sledges and carts. Mothers dreamed the hobgoblins were stifling them and moaned in their sleep, tossing fitfully among their rosy children. In the yards and stalls the oxen slept, holding the moon on their motionless horns.

And perched high on the trunk of an old elm tree, slept a pair of storks — man and wife.

Vasil and Natalka stood in a doorway. Giving themselves up in confusion and delight to the feelings that welled up inside them, they stood hand in hand, absorbed in the wonder and strangeness of the world around them. The apple tree, the willows, the

91

pots on the fences, the old elm tree — every object had become unfamiliar, taken on a quite different nocturnal shape and begun to live a life of its own. It was as if a poet had taken ordinary, everyday words, arranged them into celebratory lines, and transformed them into poetry full of new and exciting meanings.

' It's all so beautiful, isnt it? '

' Yes.'

' Vasil, why do you always ignore me in the daytime? ' Natalka asked timidly.

' But you ignore me too, don't you? '

' That's only because I'm shy. I feel somehow embarrassed in the daytime.'

' It's the same for me.'

' Really? '

' I swear. But as soon as evening comes, something draws me to you, Natalka.'

' Its the same for me. I keep thinking, if only evening would come.'

It was evening now, but they still perhaps wouldn't have summoned up the courage to put their arms round one another had not fear — woman's traditional helper — come to Natalka's assistance.

' Oh, look! ' Natalka suddenly let out a whispered shriek. ' Look, did you see? '

Somehow they found themselves in each other's arms without noticing it and they began peering into the darkness.

' How everything changes at night,' Natalka said anxiously. ' It's the willow, see? And yet it doesn't look like the willow. There's something there.'

' There's nothing there. You imagined it.'

' No, there is, something dark and furry. Can't you see? '
Natalka pressed closer to Vasil.

Vasil looked at the twisted silhouette of the old willow tree which had been half-split by lightning, but he saw nothing, nothing dark, nothing furry. He was only aware of Natalka's disturbing nearness.

' There's something evil about those old hollow willows . . . Why do they always look as if a heart's been scorched into them? Even during the day they frighten me.'

They talked about fears for a long time and both of them enjoyed the presence of this nocturnal companion of youth.

Then they parted. As they said goodbye, Vasil pressed Natalka's head to his heart and his face took on an unusually serious and thoughtful expression.

Now we see him walking home in the moonlight. There's a light dust under his feet and dew on the grass. Dark horses are grazing in the fields leaving their trace on the dew. We can make out their gleaming backs.

Something just flitted past in the shadow of the bridge behind the willow. No, it was nothing. Everything around was still — and yet not still, but full of those barely distinguishable sounds that are special to the night. Through the distant sound of girls' voices ringing softly somewhere in that silvery glow, Vasil seemed to hear the grass growing, the cucumbers sprouting, and the long pumpkin stems moving secretly through the warm steamy darkness as they curled their tendrils round the fences. He seemed to hear the cherries filling with their red juices and the peaches taking on their downy blush. The earth smelt of night flowers, of fruit and leaves, of the sweetness of sunflowers, tobacco plant and buckwheat. Everything was moving under that blue cover of life-giving night while the world slept.

In the morning at sunrise the women would come out on the porches to wash, and seeing the flowering poppies and sun-flowers still untouched by the first bee, they would exclaim in their sing-song voices: ' Lord, what's happened to the garden overnight! '

Vasil walked down the road alone. The horses snorted behind a clump of willows. He noticed them, shut his eyes and smiled at his own thoughts. The horses snorted again.

But why do we dwell on him so long? We may be well aware that the sky, the stars and the earth itself belong to him, but still, why talk about him so much? Because in five minutes he will be dead, mourned by everyone. Because these are his last steps.

But let's not be in too much of a hurry to get to that unhappy event. Let's look at him closely. He's nineteen years old. How he's grown up in this last year! His neck has thickened and strengthened, his wavy hair has taken on a shine, his strong mouth radiates health and there's the beginnings of a moustache on his upper lip. He now sings in a deep bass. His healthy arms and legs are strong and quick and he treads soundlessly, as if he moved through the air above the roads and grasses, never touching the ground with his feet. His young world is so tuned to action, so in harmony, that it sometimes seemed to him he had only to make a slight movement of the arms to rise effortlessly into the air, the way people do in dreams.

Vasil liked girls, but he still needed the armour of darkness. In daylight he was too shy to even look at them, especially on ordinary days of the week. Only those fragrant evenings, known nowhere but the Ukraine, brought him close to sweet girlish eyes.

What couldn't have come of this young Komsomol! Show him the way, give him the science, the technology, and send him where you will — as an engineer, a captain, a diplomat, an artist. Send him into battle, over mountains, to the Arctic. There's no human activity Vasil couldn't have mastered, smiling the gentle smile of his grandfather all the while.

'I feel like dancing,' Vasil thought, sensing an extraordinary lightness and joy in the movements of his body. 'How about trying a few steps, practising a bit, since no one's watching. Hey! Looks like I already know how. Like this ... and this ... and this ... (*Still*)

> *From village to village*
> *With music and dance ...*

... the words weren't important, even these old ones could do for the moment. Vasil himself was unaware that his gopak raised the dust in a fine golden cloud across the village lane. The hollow stamp of his feet and his own intense, whispered accompaniment seemed to accentuate the sleeping silence and create such a harmony between the earth and the sky that it seemed for as long as the world had existed no evil had been done in this place, nor would ever be. It wasn't the first time Vasil had improvised a dance along the sleep-laden village lanes. More than once as he danced past the huts and cottages he had roused the old people from their sleep. They even sometimes imagined they saw something through the dense hedges,

94

but since they were never sure if it was a dream or not, they would usually say the next day: 'Was that a vision I saw last night, or did I dream it, God save us? It seems to me I opened my eyes and there was someone dancing down the lane! Something out of the ordinary's going to happen!'

Vasil had now danced down three lanes. Surely this is how folk dances were born! Their joyous movements were produced, not in dancing classes on parquetry floors, but in response to the demands of overpowering emotions. They were called up, not by fiddles and trumpets, but by that inner music which obeys the immutable laws of life and fills the soul with yearning, sending the elated body leaping upwards in defiance of the laws of gravity to embrace all that is best in a man, bequeathed to him by the undying spirit of his people.

Never before had Vasil danced with such fervour. One hand behind his head, the other on his hip, he seemed to float over the village in clouds of golden dust, leaving a trail of gold curling over the quiet lanes behind him.

He was in sight of his own house. A gun shot! And Vasil was no more . . .

He fell straight out of his dance into death on the roadway. Something flitted past the willows in the distance. The horses snorted.

What a pity it is that the cinema can't speak. We are as mute as little children. Our arms reach out to grasp all sorts of useful and useless objects, we tumble, we cry and we run. Ours is a pitiful condition. And yet the time is ripe. There is so much that needs to be said. Some day people will demand to know. Who killed Vasil, the Young Communist? And why?

Instead of a cry, we will give an inscription. Let people read. But first let's cast a spell on the actor-father. Let him abandon day to day trivia and spend the night in contemplation, as if it was his own child that had been killed. Let him go out into the fields and stand grief-stricken on the hill where the roads scatter to all corners of the earth. When through the depths of grief the actor rises to transcend his muteness, only then will our inscription ring from his lips in all the languages of the world, louder than any spoken words —

'*Hear me all you Ivans, Stepans, and Grigorys* —

Did you kill my Vasil??! '

No reply. Only the telegraph wires moan sadly in the wind, spreading their sorrow over the distance.

For a long time the bereaved father stood in the field. And although there were neither precipices nor mountains around him, his head seemed to rise to the skies and the wind-driven clouds to touch his heart — his Komsomol son lay dead.

No reply. He went to the village where the streets were as usual almost deserted. He met the friends of Khoma who silently turned away. Khoma himself stood in his courtyard. He would have done better to hide in the house, but he didn't hide, he was afraid — surely the walls would fall in and crush him. Even in the yard he seemed to sway unsteadily. Wouldn't stones rain down on him from heaven?

' Was it you Khoma? '

Khoma was silent, not even raising his eyes. Opanas went up to him.

' I asked you, did you kill Vasil? '

' No, it wasn't me,' whispered Khoma, the colour left his face and a cloud passed over his pale grey eyes, making them paler still.

' It wasn't you, you say.'

' No.'

Opanas gave Khoma a long and penetrating look, then silently turned away. He sat with the coffin of his dead son for a long time, oblivious of those who came in, unaware of the tears and laments.

His simple world had been darkened and crushed by grief. Everything had stopped for him — even time. It was only a day later that he returned to himself and rose slowly to his feet, evidently having reached some decision. He looked at his dead son and at that innocent luminous smile and sadly smiled back. He was like a tired traveller returning home after a long journey. Surveying the ruins of his home in sorrow and confusion, the traveller seemed to be seeking well-loved and familiar places where nothing was recognizable any more. It was as if the ashes of what had once been had never known and would never know now the sounds of laughter, joking and good-natured disagreements.

Suddenly the door was pushed open and Natalka stood on the threshold — silhouetted against the dark passageway, she looked paler than her white blouse. But Opanas didn't see her. He only saw the open door and remembering there was somewhere he had to go, he slowly went out.

The girl was completely shattered by her loss. She looked at the boy she had shied away from in the daylight, longing for evening and the gentle sunset, and fear and grief made her hold her breath. Her parted lips were dry, and distorted in a fixed grimace as if they'd been struck by lightning. ' Vasil, my dear Vasil.' (*Still*)

She was to cry many tears into her hot pillow, spend many lonely hours with her grief. Her gentle nature was to be consumed by hatred and curses for the killer. But nothing could bring him back — everything passes. Another was destined to hold her and console her one day. It was with another that she would come to know the joy, the loves and the labours of life. Natalka leaned against Ulyana, Vasil's sister, and for a moment her strength seemed to leave her altogether.

' Where am I going? Ah yes, I remember.' Opanas made his way to Father Gerasim's, talking to himself about something all the way.

Father Gerasim was quite clearly expecting him. When Opanas crossed the threshold of his old house which reeked of age and solitude, the churchman didn't commiserate with him in his sorrow, offered no consoling words about the will of God. Mute fear flickered in Gerasim's eyes.

' There is no God, Father. No, none at all.' Opanas' voice was flat but his words were enough to fill the priest's house with thunder. ' Because if there had been a God, even if he weren't altogether almighty or all-merciful, even if he'd been a miserable little God, turned a bit senile by age and all that worship, even one like that wouldn't have let my son die that way. Go and look at him. He's lying on the table and smiling. Who is that dead man's smile meant for? Not you and me in our benighted ignorance. He was thinking about something good when he died. Well, what can you tell me, you servant of human misery? '

Father Gerasim answered not a word. In silence he lifted

trembling hands to the empty heavens to which the spiritual strength of the people had been directed for centuries in the shape of prayers, supplications and sighs.

' The conditions of life and death lead me to declare that you too don't really exist,' Opanas said quietly, and after a moment's silence the door squeaked pitifully. Father Gerasim looked around — the room was empty.

When Opanas appeared at the collective farm board head-quarters where they were discussing the event, everyone rose to their feet.

' In the life of our village...' Opanas began, breaking off abstractedly to greet the company. ' In the life of our village an event has occurred.' Opanas spoke slowly, thinking out and weighing up the meaning of each word. ' Someone found it necessary to murder my son in secret...' Opanas' flat, low voice shook slightly. ' It's because of this extraordinary event that I can assure you — our life has split in two... the life that was until his death, and the one that began from the moment when he fell to the road dead. And so that the enemy may not rejoice over his evil crime, or count to gain anything from it, I beg you... If my Vasil has died for a new life... the thought came to me as I sat by his coffin... he should be buried in a new way. I don't want priests and deacons seeing him out for a fee, but our own boys and girls with new songs about the new life. I want to conquer my sorrow.' Opanas sighed heavily. The word ' sorrow ' he uttered in a whisper.

Maksim Pritulak, the president of the farm board, and the secretary Chuprina went up to Opanas and spoke to him in voices that were as flat as his, for the same reason:

' It'll be as you say Opanas. Since your life has worked out this way and this is your wish, we'll bury our Vasil ourselves. There won't be any priests or deacons to see him off, and no dirges. There'll be no compromise! We ourselves will sing about the new life and the living Vasil.'

Need we give the words of all the songs, or describe the singers in detail, or what happened the following day when Vasil was lifted onto the shoulders of his comrades, covered to the waist by a red banner and borne on his last journey at the head of the whole village, the young and the old? The girls came with bunches of flowers, the women in white shawls carried their babies in their arms, the Komsomol wore their red ribbons, the old men had bared their heads.

It was as if people had been awakened from a long sleep by this extraordinary event and looked at the world with new eyes. The whole purpose of their existence — the hardships and misfortunes, the heroic struggles of the past, the enthusiasm of the present, the presentiment and awareness of their historic destiny — took on a single triumphant meaning.

Songs flowed into the procession from all the roads and lanes without a break like streams into a great river — old cossack and oxdrivers' refrains, songs about labour, love and the fight for freedom, and new Komsomol songs, the 'International' and the 'Testament', 'The falcon and the grey-winged eagle have joined arms. Hey! My brother and comrade!' . . . and then once more 'We'll all go into battle for the power of the Soviets'. They all flowed together into a single shattering sound. The singers embraced whole centuries of life with their songs. The brass band played triumphantly. And out of the complex inter-weaving of sounds, the collision of melodies from brass trumpets and voices, kettle drums and new songs, a popular heroic symphony was born, celebrating the triumph of the new life on earth.

Opanas followed the coffin, his eyes fixed on his son. He didn't weep, he even seemed to be smiling and whispering something, turning now and again in the direction of the singers in a gesture that was inexpressibly sad. His wife was not with him. She had obeyed the call of new life and quickly turned back while still only at the gate. Her time had come. (*Still*)

Natalka was not there either. Alone in her little summer house she tore at her clothes and flung herself against the wall, her whole body shaken with terrible sobs. Everything in her rose in anguished protest. When they carried Vasil's body past and the walls began to shake with the power of their voices, she collapsed onto the bed in the corner barely conscious.

> *Enough, grey eagle,*
> *It's time to come home.*
> *Never more, my dear one,*
> *Grief is your lot . . .*

Arkhip Belokon was riveted to the window. From the street he seemed to be suspended there on the white wall like a picture of Cain in a sombre old frame. Mouth open, hair awry, he was scarcely breathing. For the first time he felt in the depths of his being the certainty that it was no longer possible to live in the old way. What was happening to the country! Vasil Trubenko was defying death. He ran to find Khoma.

But Khoma was running, swifter than any animal. Capless, wearing only trousers and a shirt half-undone, he rushed like a madman over the fields, not knowing where. His face ran with sweat and the breath came with difficulty through his parched throat. He constantly looked from side to side as if he expected to find all the surrounding villages at his heels. What anguish filled that black mind then? Fear? Malice? A sense of doom? Or perhaps remorse for what he had done. He stopped only once in the middle of the flowering buckwheat and alone among the bees he shouted towards the village: 'I did it! I killed him! In the night, when you were all asleep! He was alone on the road — he was dancing!'

Then he turned and rushed headlong again, first in one direction, then in another, till he suddenly collapsed, burying his head in the grass and writhing like someone in the grip of fever, as if he wanted to burrow into the ground like a worm. And Vasil? When they carried him past the orchard he had loved so much, and past the sunflowers, the fruits and the flowers almost touched his clear face giving him such an expression that there were many who couldn't restrain themselves from crying out in unbearable protest. (*Still*) Then the simple words of the old oxdrivers' song rang out like thunder across the fields:

> *The oxen snorted*
> *As they plodded across the steppes,*
> *And tear flowed after tear.*
> *Can it be, dear brothers,*
> *That our comrade is with us no more?*

Other songs blended in from all sides — 'The earth belongs to us', 'The hour of reckoning is here', 'The human race will rise again', mingled with the trembling notes of the brass horn. (*Still*)

Imperceptibly clouds had begun to gather in the blue sky. They grew and multiplied, continually changing shape. Some of them looked like bearded old prophets, others like snow-covered mountains, while others raced across the sky like fantastic warrior horsemen ... Ahead of this heavenly host, its outspread wings catching the sunlight, flew an immense blue bird. Then the prophets, the battle and the bird merged into a single crow-black cloud which almost obscured the sun. As Chuprina began his speech over Vasil's grave, his red hair ruffled by gestures charged with emotion, his invocatory voice ringing like a trumpet call, the willows suddenly rustled over his head and a warm heavy rain poured down onto the sweltering, dust-covered earth. (*Still*)

There was something inexpressibly joyful and life-giving in that sunny rain, everyone felt it. It seemed to wash away the remains of grief and sorrow from people. No one looked for shelter or tried to escape the downpour. The children even lifted their faces to it and chanted: ' Rain, rain, go away, come again another day ...'

The orchards and vegetable patches, melon fields and meadows were soon rain-washed. Drops slid over the smooth, shining surfaces of the apples and plums to hang suspended for a moment before overflowing onto the ground. (*Still*)

This is where our film ends. It is only the things that are beautiful in a man's life, or in the lives of whole generations of men, that survive after death. Arkhip Belokon's race soon disappeared without leaving a trace, while Vasil Trubenko still lives on in popular tradition — only the sadness and regret has died, giving way to gratitude.

People remember his light tread, his smile, and all the things he could do so quickly and cheerfully. Songs have been written about him. There is just old man Opanas, a team-leader in the collective now, who still weeps for his beloved son at night sometimes, stifling his sobs with his cap so as not to frighten the nightingale in the cherry tree.

The nightingales sing in the young orchards. You can hear choirs of girls' voices in the distance. The kolkhoz lands are blooming as never before. Old man Petro has won his peace and lies beside his friend in the graveyard. And Natalka has found happiness with another, and consolation with him in their work and their children.